JAPANESE RELIGIONS:
PAST AND PRESENT

JAPANESE RELIGIONS
Past and Present

Ian Reader,
Esben Andreasen &
Finn Stefánsson

UNIVERSITY OF HAWAII PRESS
HONOLULU

JAPANESE RELIGIONS: PAST & PRESENT

Published in North America by
University of Hawaii Press
2840 Kolowalu Street
Honolulu, Hawaii 96822

Reprinted 1995

Published in Great Britain by
Japan Library/Curzon Press Ltd
Knoll House, 35 The Crescent
Sandgate
Folkestone, Kent CT20 3EE

Printed in England

Library of Congress Cataloging-in-Publication Data

Reader, Ian, 1949-
    Japanese religions: past and present/by Ian Reader, with Esben
Andreasen [sic], Finn Stefánsson.
        p. cm.
    '...originally written and published in Danish by Esben Andreasen
and Finn Stefánsson. It has been thoroughly revised for English
publication by these authors and Ian Reader...'-Pref.
    Includes bibliographical references and index.
    ISBN 0-8248-1545-9. - ISBN 0-8248-1546-7 (pbk.)
    1. Japan - Religion. I. Andreasen, Esben. II. Stefánsson, Finn,
1942-. III. Title.
BL2202.R43 1993
200'.952-dc20   93-2725
                                                                     CIP

Set in Goudy Old Style Medium 11 on 12 point.
by Visual Typesetting, Harrow, Middlesex.
Keywork by Ann Tiltman
Printed in England by BPC Wheatons Ltd., Exeter.

Contents

5

6. The New Religions of Japan

7. Christianity in Japan

CONTENTS

8. Religion and Politics in Japan

Attribution
Every effort has been made to contact the copyright holders of the extracts and photographs that appear in this book; where it has not been possible to do so, the publishers apologise for any inconvenience caused.

Preface

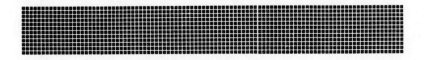

This book was originally published in Danish by Esben Andreasen and Finn Stefánsson. It has been thoroughly revised for publication in English by these authors and Ian Reader, who has written several new sections, updated the materials and provided the linking commentaries and introductions to the chapters. In both content and presentation it has been prepared as an introductory guide to the religious traditions of Japan as they are today together with some background information on their historical development.

The book is divided into eight chapters, each of which deals with a specific topic relevant to Japanese religions. Apart from Chapter Two, which offers a general overview of religion in Japan, each chapter consists of an introduction that outlines the topic to be dealt with, followed by a series of complementary readings. The opening commentary in each chapter contextualises the readings and outlines and explains the themes that they contain.

In all there are 50 readings in the book, taken from both Japanese and Western language sources. In an attempt to present a balanced picture we have used the writings of academics who are experts in the study of Japanese religions, as well as Japanese texts and the writings of Japanese religious organisations. The chapters relate to each other, but each is also designed to be read as a unit in itself, with the readings expanding on and giving life to the points made in the introduction.

It is essential, when studying any religion to know something of the culture from which it sprang, and the purpose of Chapter One is to provide some information on this issue. The chapter examines Japan academically through readings on Japanese social relations, cultural patterns of behaviour and language, and also provides views of what life in Japan is all about as seen through the eyes of visitors. Chapter Two continues with further background information and provides a general overview, with a brief historical outline, of religion in Japan and of the various religious traditions that are found there.

Chapters Three, Four, Five, Six and Seven examine some of the influential religions and religious customs and traditions of Japan. In Chapter Three we encounter the world of Japanese folk religion, along with some commonly-held beliefs, ideas and customs, and see how these still play a part in Japanese life today. Chapter Four focuses on one of the main organised religions in Japan, the ethnic and national religion, Shinto, while Chapter Five looks at Buddhism, a religion that originally entered Japan over 1400 years ago but which has become established as the other major organised Japanese religious tradition along with Shinto.

In Chapter Six we meet the most actively growing religious phenomenon in Japan over the past century - the new religions. Many hundreds of new religions have grown - and continue to grow - in twentieth-century Japan, and this chapter provides an insight into these new religions, their teachings and activities. Chapter Seven turns to a religious tradition from the West, Christianity, that first appeared over four centuries ago in Japan. Christianity remains numerically a minority religion in Japan yet, as this chapter shows, it has none the less made some impact. This chapter looks both at the influences Christianity has had in Japan as well as looking at reasons why it still remains a minority religion.

The last chapter looks at one important, recurrent and often controversial theme in Japanese religious history, the relationship between religion and politics, and between religion and the state. In particular, it deals with the position of the Emperor of Japan, and with the relationship of religion, politics and the state in the period leading up to the Second World War, when Shinto was supported as a state religion, and the period since the war, when religion has become officially separate from the state.

Notes on the readings as well as a short introductory bibliography are provided at the end of the book for the benefit of those who want to pursue this subject further. We very much hope you will.

1
Meeting Japanese Culture

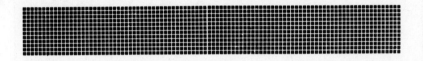

Over the past century and a half, and especially in the decades since 1945, Japanese society has undergone some of the most rapid changes that any society has ever seen. From 1853, when Japan was opened up to the outside world by the Americans, until the end of the nineteenth century, the Japanese saw their country transformed from a feudal society into an industrialised one, heavily influenced by the West. Japanese political and education systems were based on Western models, while modern Western techniques in industry, engineering, manufacturing and many other fields were swiftly learned and assimilated. In the early twentieth century Japan began to come into conflict with other countries, first with Russia, which she defeated in war in 1904-5, and later with China and, of course, the Allies in the Second World War.

The twentieth century has been, in many respects, one of turbulence for Japan: wars, industrial upheavals, the strife of industrial recessions and depressions in the 1920s and 1930s, the emergence of an increasingly nationalistic and fascist regime and the years of military expansion from the early 1930s on, leading to total war. Japan became the only nation to experience the horrors of atomic bombs at first hand, at Hiroshima and Nagasaki in 1945, and shortly after, beaten, desolate and in chaos, for the first time in her history had to submit to defeat at the hands of foreign powers.

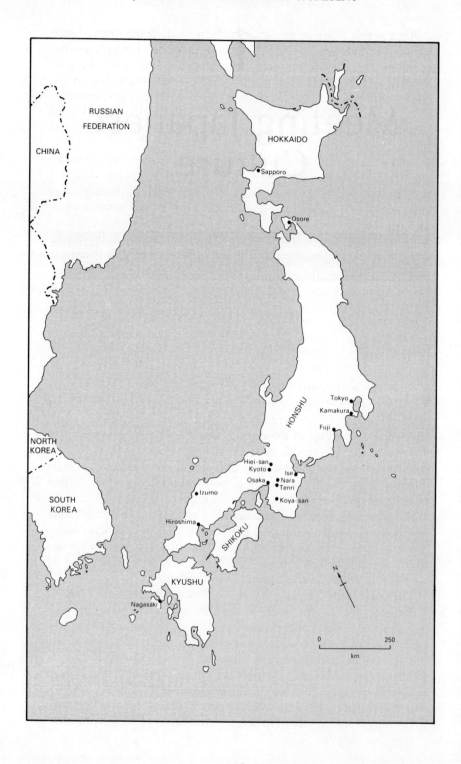

After seven years of foreign rule by an occupying army, Japan returned to independence in 1952, and since then her progress has been staggering. The desolate wastelands of 1945 have become hi-tech bustling cities, and the Japanese economy has risen, phoenix-like, to make Japan one of the world's richest nations. Japan today is a world leader, an industrial and technological giant to whom the West now looks for inspiration and for new goods and ideas.

All this has had a considerable effect on the lives of the Japanese, who have become, in a few decades, a race of city-dwelling industrialists where they were once village-dwelling farmers. Yet one of the most remarkable features of Japanese life is that, while so much has changed, there remains a sense of underlying stability, both in the social system and within Japanese culture. The religious ethos itself has been a major influence here: as the first chapter shows, there is a sense of continuity that has helped give people a source of strength and stability which acts as a balance to the increasing speed of change in other aspects of life. These underlying continuities will become more apparent in subsequent chapters.

The readings in this chapter will also bring out some of those underlying stabilities whilst providing the outsider with an introduction to Japanese culture in general. Reading No. 1 is an impressionistic view of Japan by a Western observer which brings out many of the differences between Japan and the West that strike visitors to Japan. It also draws attention to many of the cultural elements of stability in Japan (the important adherence to concepts of purity, ceremony, style and ritual, for example). Some of these themes appear, in a different way, in the next reading (No. 2) on Japanese language. In order to understand a culture it is useful to at least have some knowledge of the ways its language functions. Aasulv Lande's introduction to the complexities and intricacies of the Japanese language helps us in this, for it shows the flexible nature of Japanese, able to assimilate elements from abroad, as well as the ways it underpins and provides a sense of cultural stability.

In particular it brings out the importance in Japan of relationships between people, an issue that is developed by the next two readings. Harumi Befu (No. 3) discusses key elements in Japanese cultural behaviour, ethics and social relationships. Ruth Benedict (No. 4) looks at some of these issues from a different angle, and her analysis of Japan as a 'shame' rather than as a 'guilt' culture (an idea presented in her famous work The Chrysanthemum and the Sword, published in 1946) has been a central question in the continuing debate on the nature of the Japanese national character. In the final reading, Takeo Doi (No. 5) discusses and expands on this issue further, relating it to some of the key cultural issues of obligation discussed by Befu, and providing a generally sympathetic Japanese response to and discussion of Benedict's ideas. The themes found in these readings, concerning Japanese social attitudes, ethics and social relationships, provide some of the basic foundations of Japanese culture. At the same time they express many of the themes that are important within Japanese religious culture as well, and as such will be addressed in various contexts throughout the rest of this book.

□□□□

Reading No. 1
Japan - the pure land: the impressions of a visitor

By FINN STEFÁNSSON

Everything is so pure, so neat, so decorative - like a doll's house. The chairs are too small, the seats in the coach are not so big either, again and again you have to bend to enter a door. The rice paddies are small like the squares on a chessboard, the rooms are like cells in a honeycomb, the rush hours in Tokyo are claustrophobic.

The Westerner towers like a giant, especially among elderly Japanese. The youth have begun to grow taller because of the more varied diet after the Second World War. It will not be long before the average height of the Japanese reaches that of the people from Northern Europe.

In many fields the Japanese are ahead of us, especially in technology. Everywhere you see the effects of highly advanced computer-controlled technology. Buses and trains depart, not to the minute, but to the second. Japan's superb public transport, spear-headed by the ultra-fast 'hikari' (bullet) service on Japan's new inter-city network (Shinkansen) is perhaps the best in the world.

Rice growing in Hokkaido

Buses and commercial vehicles in reverse gear automatically give out warning sounds. At pedestrian crossings, the green light is accompanied by music to let the blind know when to cross.

In the car factories industrial robots attack the steel plates like prehistoric lizards, greedy and fire-breathing, and each may carry out five or six complicated processes along the assembly line. Live 'industrial robots' then carry out a similar series of processes.

The reverse side of Japanese efficiency is a certain automation and uniformity. What are these live robots who dedicate their lives to the factories like in real life? Why do schoolchildren wear old-fashioned, black uniforms? Why must boys of 10 to 14 have crew-cut hair styles like soldiers? Why do the vast majority of males living in the cities wear dark suits and ties? Why do people on underground trains and on buses sleep as if remote-controlled?

At once foreign yet familiar to us, Japan is a welfare state with shops abounding in goods. Prices are higher than in Western countries but the range of goods often surpasses anything we see in cities in the West.

Foreign to us are, for instance, the code of politeness, people's shyness and the central concepts of purity.

The mixture of shyness and politeness is ingrained from childhood. Again and again you meet groups of schoolchildren coming towards you, curious but also shy. They titter and draw back a little when you say hello, but then their curiosity prevails.

15

You shake hands and again this is almost too much. They withdraw from you until finally, when they have reached a certain distance, they wave and shout, 'Goodbye' - more and more hilariously the further they retreat. This tittering shyness applies to almost all women - they bow submissively and shrink back in the same movement.

The themes of purity and purification are constantly on view in Japan. At all Shinto shrines there are places of purification, and this ritual purification gives purity to body and soul which leads to honesty. A key concept in Japanese ethics is *shōjiki* ('there are no lies'). Through purification the connection to the divine is restored, and all existence is revived by being taken back to its original plane and source. The life of a Japanese is to be compared to the cycle of the sun: sunset means purification in water, sunrise means revival. The daily visit to the shrine is thus deeply ingrained into the course of nature. It also means that important European concepts such as the conflict between the divine and man (sin) and between soul and body (dualism) do not exist in the Japanese world.

The symbolism of renewal and resurrection can be found in a peculiar tradition at the great Shinto shrines at Ise. The extremely beautiful main shrine, built of wood, is replaced every twentieth year by a new, exact copy of the old, erected on a purified site next to the old. The extensive re-building symbolises the purification and revival of all of Japan. Standing at the site under the cedars, 50 metres high, a thousand years old, and planted when the first gracefully simple shrine was erected, one can sense this feeling of continued renewal.

Purity also means being able to distinguish between different spatial relations, such as inside and outside. When you enter a house you take off your shoes at the front door and put on a pair of slippers (usually too small!) You must not wear any kind of shoes on the *tatami* mats in the inner apartment; in the toilet there is a pair of toilet slippers; and if you go to the small pavilion in the garden, you wear outdoor slippers, and having arrived at the pavilion, you change these into pavilion slippers. It may sound like a comic ritual but it definitely gives you a heightened awareness of where you are. It is a mixture of prim stylisation and sublime aesthetics.

The traditional Japanese way of life is ceremonial and stylised, and reveres beauty in the minutest details. The aesthetics, built on a harmonious fusion of disparate forms, is expressed in the tea ceremony, in all sorts of cooking, sports, dress, gardening, the wrapping paper used for gifts, ink calligraphy and the various artistic forms such as *ikebana* (flower arrangement).

The concepts of purity entail some serious drawbacks:

discrimination against people with impure jobs and of people belonging to ethnic minorities has long been a problem in Japan. Blood, dead animals and human excrement have long been seen as impure and therefore taboo subjects. As a result, butchers, tanners, street sweepers and refuse collectors have for centuries been seen as marginal members of society. At the bottom of the social pyramid there is a group known as the *burakumin*, estimated at two to three million people, whose social status is comparable to the untouchables of India. In the Tokugawa period, when the hierarchic structure prevailed, this group was called 'people who are not people' and even today they are considered a race apart by many Japanese who feel that to mention them is taboo.

Similarly these ideas about the purity of the race discriminate against the *Ainu*, the aborigines of the northern Island of Hokkaido, and the many Koreans (whose culture paradoxically has influenced the Japanese very much) who have been resident in Japan for many years yet still are marginalised in Japanese society.

SHRINES, TEMPLES AND FESTIVALS

It was an aesthetic experience of the highest order to stroll around amidst the temples and shrines in the two ancient capitals of Nara and Kyoto. Kyoto alone has about 2000 temples and shrines, and each compound contains groups of buildings and gardens. The Kiyomizu temple was especially impressive: the sweeping lines of

Main hall of Kiyomizu Temple, Kyoto

17

beautiful wooden buildings, some on pillars, situated in a landscape with glowing autumn colours so that buildings and nature formed one whole. It is a national treasure and museum but is also still in use as a temple, with thousands of visitors, especially schoolchildren, who amuse themselves studying the oracles they have just bought, and pray to ask the gods to help them in their school work and their relationships, and to make their family life prosperous.

The most delightful experience I had was at a Shinto festival, a *matsuri*, celebrating fertility. It took place in a small town of about 15,000 inhabitants, just over 100 miles south of Tokyo. The whole town was full of excitement. Carts, perhaps five metres high, bearing children and musicians, were drawn by ropes to various parts of the town. There were planned stops on the route until a certain drum beat, the regular shouts - *wasshoi, wasshoi* - and archaic flute playing once more got the pullers, dressed in their festival clothes, moving again. Perhaps we were the first Europeans who had seen this particular *matsuri*: certainly we were given an extremely generous reception. We were given festival clothes, lots of saké and beer, the children in the carts stretched down to touch us, and we were asked to pull the ropes. Heeling over and swaying, sometimes dangerously close to telephone poles and houses, the carts were pulled through the narrow streets. We were like carts ourselves, staggering along looking over the Lilliputian houses, Gullivers in wonderland.

*　　*　　*

IN A LECTURE Professor Takenaka from the Christian Doshisha University, Kyoto, summed up three central points in Japanese culture:

First of all Japan is an *ohayo*-culture, a 'good morning' culture. *Ohayo* really means 'early in the morning', and is used by the farming population who start working early in the fields. But the expression is deeply rooted in the Japanese mentality and projects the Confucian ethics of: you must work hard, be honest and obedient.

Another aspect of the expression deals with man's relationship to nature: you say good morning to nature, which is not an object, but a fellow being, a subject you can communicate with. There is no distance, no master-slave relationship. The moon is your friend to whom you can turn and who can turn to you: 'Good morning, how are you? It was cold last night'.

This closeness to nature can also be found in the finely-tuned appreciation of the seasons. In all ceremonies, in *haiku* poems, in gastronomy - everywhere the four seasons are to be found. Snow, cherry blossoms, the bloom of iris and lotus, and the colourful leaves

Deer at the Todaiji Temple, Nara

of maples in autumn - these are the four seasons, *shiki*.

Professor Takenaka added that the divine cannot be defined, debated and rationalised as in European culture. There is no difference between god, nature and man: 'God means that in spite of the cold winter life goes on'.

Secondly, Japan is a *furusato*-culture, an 'old or native village' culture. *Furusato* is where people live long together and traditions are born. Here you are in harmony with religions, nature and society. New elements are absorbed into this culture, for instance Buddhism, in such a way that they become part of fundamental tradition. 'It works well for us, so why not adopt it?' is the basic thinking behind this.

After the loss of the village community, when two or three generations ago the Japanese moved into the cities, a great many people have become 'homeless'. The fellowship provided in the new religions is a substitute for the solidarity in the old *furusato* for many people.

The last point, *sayonara*, is the Japanese farewell greeting, which really means: 'If so, let it be so'. Life is like a stream. Maybe you

19

want the lovely autumn day you are enjoying together to last forever, but now we must part. Let it be so.

The positive aspect of *sayonara* is acceptance of the conditions of life, the negative aspect a propensity to resignation and avoidance of problems.

These three points are closely related to the Japanese concept of man. The word for human being means 'person together with', which signifies that our individualism does not exist in Japanese language and mentality. There you find 'betweenness', relationship, community, fellowship - with your neighbour, the nation, nature. Time/history is 'time together', space is 'room together'.

This culture of relationships is also seen in what is distinctive. When a Japanese painter paints bamboo plants, for instance, half of the picture is empty and it is this emptiness which adds interest to the painting.

Void and fullness, emptiness and form, are genuine Zen terms. At Kyoto National Museum I saw an exhibition of Japanese paintings from about 1600-1800. Sophisticated stylisations of landscapes with small waterfalls and teeming with birds: sparrows, swans, the veiled face of the moon above the reeds, a solitary bamboo and no more - these paintings were miles 'ahead' of contemporary European art. Not until the nineteenth century have 'we' been able to paint like that - almost.

Five groups of small rocks placed in white gravel, meticulously raked: this is one of the most famous spots in Japan - the Zen garden at Ryoanji, Kyoto. Again what is distinctive is simplicity, stylisation, emptiness. The void fills up or is filled.

Darkness falls on the lotus pond at Ryoanji while the maples glow around it. Walking home to my temporary lodgings up Mount Hiei I get an impressionist-stylised experience: a dark blue night, the dizzy song of cicadas, the moon like a veiled ship above Hiei-zan, the mountain that towers over and protects Kyoto.

Reading No. 2
The Japanese language

By AASULV LANDE

Japanese calligraphy: *So saku hyo gen* ('creation' or 'expression')

Japanese is not closely related to any other language and so is generally considered to be an independent language. The structure of the language is somewhat similar to Korean, Mongolian and Turkish, but there is no close connection. There are words that Chinese, Korean and Japanese have in common, and usually this is due to Chinese influence. From at least the fifth century, and perhaps earlier, Chinese words and written language have entered Japanese.

The first written language adopted by the Japanese was Chinese, which is very different from Japanese. Whereas Japanese has numerous inflexions Chinese words have no inflected forms. However, because the Japanese did not have a written language of their own, they adopted the Chinese system, and from the eighth century began producing literary texts using Chinese characters.

The adopted Chinese symbols were later transformed and modified by use of phonetic systems called *katakana* and *hiragana*, which the Japanese developed in the ninth century. These are used today together with Chinese characters.

There is a particular problem, however, that Chinese characters have many readings in Japanese. The character 上 ,for instance,has the readings *kami, ue* and *jo*, but also several other readings, all dependent on the context.

Another problem is the fact that many Chinese words are pronounced alike in Japanese. So the same words in phonetic script may mean various things. The main English language Japanese character dictionary gives 62 characters, each of which are pronounced as *shin*. Some of the most frequent meanings of *shin* are:

- god
- heart, mind
- new
- true

This ambivalence is part of the language structure and influences communication in Japan. For instance it is common to see Japanese gesticulating in order to emphasise what sign they are referring to when the sounds are ambiguous.

There are about 2000 characters that are in standard everyday use in Japan, and that have to be learned. Learning them is one of the major tasks of Japanese schoolchildren, and one of the major elements in the Japanese education system. Learning all these characters is laborious work involving writing and repetition, and in any Japanese class there are always some who find it very difficult to learn all the characters properly. A lot of extra time is also needed to keep up one's knowledge.

In certain periods, for instance during the modernisation of Japan around the turn of the century and after the war in 1945, there were influential groups working on replacing the Japanese written language by the Latin alphabet. But other arguments have carried greater weight for the Japanese than an efficient system of letters. Such arguments emphasise linguistic identity and tradition, the common linguistic heritage of East Asia and the difficulties of substituting a complete system of communication with a new one.

SENTENCE STRUCTURE

A basic Japanese sentence has two parts called topic (T) and comment (C). The topic usually ends with the particle *wa*. This particle connects the topic to the following comment (C). The comment is the most important part whereas the topic is largely a modifier. So the topic is an attribute which can be left out without altering the overall meaning. Often the subject of the sentence in Japanese may be left out, and be implied only.

Let us look at a Japanese sentence and analyse it into topic (T) and comment (C):

Tarosan wa	_maiasa_	_uchi kara_	_gakko made_	_basu de_	_ikimasu_
T	A	B	C	D	H
Mr Taro	each-morning	house-from	school-to	bus-with	go

(Each morning Mr Taro takes the bus from his home to the school)

H is in reality the main part of the sentence. It is enough to say this part and thus point to the process of going. ABCD modifies this and together with H they constitute the comment (C). The topic (T) finally modifies the built-up and modified main part.

$$\boxed{T} \rightarrow A\rightarrow \boxed{\boxed{B} \rightarrow \boxed{\boxed{C} \rightarrow \boxed{H}}}$$

(A   B   C   D .... H)

Compared to Western languages the Japanese language structure is characteristically personal. That means that personal relations (superiority - coordination - subordination) are reflected in the language.

'To go' is _iku_ (normal infinitive): connected to the verbal ending _masu_ it becomes _ikimasu_, a formal and polite level of the verb. The sentence about Mr Taro, above, has this style. If you are to express other people's 'goings' in even more polite forms you can do so by using _irassharu_ which combined with the formal verb _masu_ becomes _irasshaimasu_. This word has a very polite and respectful ring to it. But there is even more respect in the alternative _oide ni narimasu_. And politeness may be emphasised by adding deferential endings to the personal name. Taro_san_ is standard politeness, whereas Taro_kun_ is informal or has a subordinate ring. Taro_chan_ is used about small children. To say Taro and no more would in most instances be directly impolite or derogatory. On the contrary, forms like Taro_sama_ or Taro_dono_ are extremely polite, and the last form - _dono_ - is strongly formal.

What is said about the way you talk about others also goes for the way you address others. But if you are talking about yourself, other rules apply, and one should use humble or deferential terms. Here a form like _ikimasu_ would be normal and is the formal expression used in educated speech. But by using forms like _ukagau_ + _masu_ = _ukagaimasu_ the expression becomes submissive. To use this verb in this form about oneself is to express submissive respect. Submissiveness and other forms of personal relations can also find expression in the choice of different personal pronouns. Using *watakushi* when talking about yourself is extremely polite. Words like *boku* (also 'I') are informal and used among friends, whereas the word *ore* (a less formal word for 'I') in some connections has a vulgar ring. *Boku* and *ore* are only used by males.

To make use of ambiguity is another way of being polite. The word *irassharu*, mentioned earlier as a polite form of 'to go', also means 'to come' or 'to be'. Ambiguity entails diffusion which creates a good, polite atmosphere. The same goes for *ukagau* which also means 'to go' and 'to ask'.

Vagueness is polite. This is true also when leaving out a direct subject. The indistinctness that arises by not expressing the subject, but implying it, is understood as being polite. Thus it is easily understandable that in Japan there is a great difference between the way women and men speak, and that there are large differences in the levels of politeness. This increases the capacity of the language to show respect to others and to create a warm, or sometimes a derogatory, atmosphere. It is not a democratic characteristic but it opens up the way for the expression of many emotional values.

The word for human beings is *ningen* 人間 In reality the word means 'between people'. In other words human beings are relational, and become human beings only together with human beings. In a flash you realise that this culture is not individualistic but social at its deepest layers, concerned primarily with the relationships between people.

Japanese is a language that, like Japanese society and culture itself, is concerned with the ways people relate together. It also expresses a sense of aesthetics, both in the shape of the characters used themselves, and in the levels of formal politeness that are so intrinsic to Japanese culture. At the same time it is a language - and a culture - ready to adapt and change: the Japanese are quick to assimilate foreign words into their language and give them an interestingly Japanese twist. The word for a personal computer in Japanese is *pasokon*, for strike *sutoraiki*, and there are countless other foreign loanwords in daily use.

Japanese is a difficult language because of the levels of politeness and the large number of characters that must be learned. However, to learn it opens many doors to Japanese culture, and is a fascinating journey in itself.

Reading No. 3
Normative values:
On, Giri, Ninjō

By HARUMI BEFU

A maid secretly hands a letter to a courtesan and
at the same time whispers in her mistresses ear.
Woodblock by Utamaru

Although many Japanese nowadays disclaim the significance of
the traditional values [*on, giri* and *ninjō*], calling them by the
epithet 'feudalistic', their own behaviour patterns betray social
relations which can best be described in terms of these concepts.

On

We shall start with the concept of *on* because the other concepts
can be analysed in relation to it. *On* is, first of all, indebtedness,

which arises from receiving some resource which one needs but does not have. Second, dispensation of this resource is clearly institutionalised. That is, there are socially expected relationships which demand dispensation of resources, for example, parents nurturing their children and *oyabun* looking after the welfare of his *kobun*. Such dispensation, however, need not be required by law; in fact, the sense of indebtedness is strengthened because the resource is given without external legal compulsion forced upon the dispensing agent. In the early feudal period, when the concept of *on* was beginning to be institutionalised, the most critical resource to be dispensed was land, which vassals received as a reward for their loyalty to their lord. Third, the giver and receiver of the debt are in a particularistic relationship - one which is meaningful only because the giver is a particular individual to the receiver and vice versa. However, two individuals who are not in such a relationship to begin with may become an *on*-giver and an *on*- receiver, e.g., when a stranger saves another's life. In such a case, a particularistic relationship is expected to develop between the two.

Fourth, the *on*-giver and *on*-receiver are in hierarchical relation. A hierarchical relationship is built on power and authority. Fifth, the *on* relationship assumes that the debt created by dispensation of the *on* will be returned.

Although *on* is a normative concept, it has a psychological basis which should not be difficult to understand. The genesis of the *on* relationship is found in the parent-child relationship, where parents give life to the child, nurture him, and socialise him. The child is then forever indebted to the parents, and the child's behaviour patterns, which are directed toward returning this debt, are what is indicated by the concept of filial piety (*oya kōkō*).

This pattern of relationships is then transferred later in life to persons other than parents. And to the extent that a similar psychological bond and mutual dependence develop between the two individuals, one feels compelled to repay the debt.

It is at this juncture that the concept of loyalty (*chū*) enters. At the normative level, loyalty is an expression of returning *on* to one's master, lord, or the Emperor, and is essentially the same as filial piety in quality. It is important to note that these two normative concepts, filial piety and loyalty, imply the same thing in substance. The readiness with which Japanese can move from the kinship context to other social contexts has had crucial implications for Japan's modernisation.

Ideally, in loyalty situations, as in parent-child relations, there should be, as there generally was in the traditional period, a particularistic relationship between the superior and the subordinate, so that a psychological bond which had developed in the parent-child relationship could be transferred. In short, loyalty was not a generalised concept that involved being loyal to a principle or to the nation or state, but a relationship holding between two specific individuals. In the modern period, however, Japanese political leaders extended the concept to apply to one's relation to the nation and the emperor.

Although such traditional concepts as *on* and repayment of debts are often said to be dying out and no longer important, a nation-wide survey conducted as late as 1968 indicated that these concepts are far from being dead. Respondents were asked to choose two important items out of the following four: *oya-kōkō*, repaying debt (*on*), respect for individual rights, and respect for freedom. The largest percentage chose *oya-kōkō*. The other three were chosen in about the same proportion. Thus one can say that filial piety is still a very powerful concept and that the concept of *on* is no less important than the more modern concepts of individual rights and freedom.

Giri

Giri, which may be translated as 'social obligation', is a normative or ethical imperative requiring Japanese to behave as expected by the society in relation to another individual with whom one is in some meaningful, or particularistic relationship. It is important to note that as in the case of *on* and loyalty, the concept of *giri* is applicable to particular persons not to just any individual.

But *giri* is a broader concept in that it also applies to egalitarian social relations where individuals are not in a hierarchical relationship, e.g., between friends, neighbours, and relatives. Behaving properly in an agalitarian context — observing gift-giving etiquette, providing labour services in an agricultural community when expected, etc. — is regarded as observing one's obligation, or *giri*. A breach of this obligation is a breach of the moral codes of society and results in sanctions of various kinds and degrees. People will lose trust and confidence in such a person as a moral individual. Although *giri* is a concept which became institutionalised in the feudal past, it can be applied to modern Japanese society and still serves as an important motivational force in social interaction. In short, *giri* is the normative force which attempts to maintain social institutions in a smooth-running condition, irrespective of how an individual might feel about the social order or about other persons with whom he must interact.

Ninjō

The moral compulsion implied by *giri* is important also in contrasting

27

it with the concept of *ninjō*, a person's 'natural' inclinations, feelings, and desires. Whereas *giri* is social and moral, *ninjō* is psychological and personal. It is entirely possible for a person's private feelings to be in complete accord with what the society dictates. One may truly wish, for example, to marry the person selected by one's parents and be happy with the marriage. But it is not likely that the private feelings of all members of a society, no matter how well integrated, are in harmony with social demands.

The discrepancy between what is expected of individuals by the society and what one wishes to do is the dilemma between *giri* and *ninjō* which has been made so often the theme of *belle-lettres* in traditional and modern Japan. There is no satisfactory resolution of this dilemma. To honour the society's ethical codes requires suppression of one's feelings; but succumbing to *ninjō* will cause social censure. Caught in this dilemma, there are three alternatives: one, to suppress one's private feelings and honour moral principles; two, to close one's eyes to moral obligations and follow the dictates of one's feeling; and three, to annihilate oneself through committing suicide, being able neither to ignore the society's moral obligations nor suppress one's personal desires. It is this third alternative which many Japanese have chosen and which has been dealt with in modern and traditional stories, attesting to the power of moral compulsion in Japanese society.

Reading No. 4
Shame cultures and guilt cultures

By RUTH BENEDICT

In anthropological studies of different cultures the distinction between those which rely heavily on shame and those that rely heavily on guilt is an important one. A society that inculcates absolute standards of morality and relies on men's developing a conscience is a guilt culture by definition, but a man in such a society may, as in the United States, suffer in addition from shame when he accuses himself of gaucheries which are in no way sins. He may be exceedingly chagrined about not dressing appropriately for the occasion or about a slip of the tongue.

In a culture where shame is a major sanction, people are chagrined about acts which we expect people to feel guilty about. This chagrin can be very intense and it cannot be relieved, as guilt can be, by confession and atonement. A man who has sinned can get relief by unburdening himself. This device of confession is used in our secular therapy and by many religious groups which have otherwise little in common. We know it brings relief. Where shame is the major sanction, a man does not experience relief when he makes his fault public even to a confessor. So long as his bad behaviour does not 'get out into the world' he need not be troubled and confession appears to him merely a way of courting trouble. Shame cultures therefore do not provide for confessions, even to the gods. They have ceremonies for good luck rather than for expiation.

True shame cultures rely on external sanctions for good behaviour, not, as true guilt cultures do, on an internalised conviction of sin. Shame is a reaction to other people's criticism. A man is shamed either by being openly ridiculed and rejected or by fantasying to himself that he has been made ridiculous. In either case it is a potent sanction. But it requires an audience or at least a man's fantasy of an audience. Guilt does not. In a nation where honour means living up to one's own picture of oneself, a man may suffer from guilt though no man knows of his misdeed and a man's feeling of guilt may actually be relieved by confessing his sin.

The early Puritans who settled in the United States tried to base their whole morality on guilt and all psychiatrists know what trouble contemporary Americans have with their consciences. But shame is an increasingly heavy burden in the United States and guilt is less extremely felt than in earlier generations. In the United States this is interpreted as a relaxation of morals. There is much truth in this, but that is because we do not expect shame to do the heavy work of morality. We do not harness the acute personal chagrin which accompanies shame to our fundamental system of morality.

The Japanese do. A failure to follow their explicit sign-posts of good behaviour, a failure to balance obligations or to foresee contingencies is a shame (haji). Shame, they say, is the root of virtue. A man who is sensitive to it will carry out all the rules of good behaviour. 'A man who knows shame' is sometimes translated 'virtuous man', sometimes 'man of honour'. Shame has the same place of authority in Japanese ethics that 'a clear conscience', 'being right with God', and the avoidance of sin have in Western ethics.

29

Logically enough, therefore, a man will not be punished in the afterlife.

The Japanese - except for priests who know the Indian sutras - are quite unacquainted with the idea of reincarnation dependent upon one's merit in this life, and - except for some well-instructed Christian converts - they do not recognise post-death reward and punishment or a heaven and a hell.

□□□□

Reading No. 5
Sin and shame

By TAKEO DOI

Ever since Ruth Benedict first distinguished two principal cultural patterns based respectively on the sense of guilt and the sense of shame and cited Japanese culture as the typical example of the latter, most foreign students of Japan seem, despite a certain amount of criticism from Japanese scholars, to have accepted her theory. I myself am on the whole disposed to side with her, but more for what we have learned through the sensitivity of her feeling for the Japanese psychology than from any desire to swallow her theories whole. They raise, in fact, a considerable number of questions, not the least of which is the fact that she allows value judgements to creep into her ideas. Specifically, it is evident that when she states that the culture of guilt places emphasis on inner standards of conduct whereas the culture of shame places emphasis on outward standards of conduct she has the feeling that the former is superior to the latter.

A second difficulty is that she seems to postulate guilt and shame as entirely unrelated to each other, which is obviously contrary to the facts. One and the same person very often experiences these two emotions at the same time, and they would seem to have a very close relationship; the person who has committed a 'sin' is very frequently ashamed of what he has done. Nevertheless, the impression still remains that in characterising Japanese culture as a culture of shame she has pointed out something extremely important, and in what follows I shall examine this point in greater detail.

Let us first examine the fact that in Western eyes the Japanese sense of guilt appears to be rather sluggish. The reason is probably that where the Westerner tends to think of the sense of guilt as an inner problem for the individual, the Japanese has no such idea. It would be foolish, of course, to assume that the Japanese have no sense of guilt. What is characteristic about the Japanese sense of guilt, though, is that it shows itself most sharply when the individual suspects that his action will result in betraying the group to which he belongs.

Even with the Western sense of guilt one might, in fact, postulate a deep-lying psychology of betrayal, but the Westerner is not normally conscious of it. What probably happened is that in the course of centuries of exposure to Christian teachings, the group - which almost certainly played an important part in his moral outlook at first - was gradually replaced by God, who in turn faded away with the advent of the modern age, leaving the individul awareness to carry on by itself. Since psychoanalytic opinion holds that the Western sense of guilt arises as a result of going against a super-ego that forms in the inner mind, the element of betrayal would seem not to have disappeared entirely. However, although his super-ego, being defined as a function of the inner mind, may well include individual personal elements such as influences from the parents, its nature is, even so, essentially impersonal. In the Western sense of guilt the sense of betrayal remains only as a trace, and is no longer experienced strongly as such.

With the Japanese, on the other hand, the sense of guilt is most strongly aroused when, as we have seen, the individual betrays the trust of the members of his own group. One could express this differently by saying that the sense of guilt is a function of human relations. For example, in the case of relatives who are most close to him, and parents in particular, the individual does not usually have much sense of guilt, presumably because both sides are so close that *amae* gives confidence of any sin being forgiven. What does often happen, though, is that the sense of guilt hitherto suppressed is felt following a parent's death - as is expressed by the saying that 'one realises one's *on* to one's parents after they are dead'.

Generally speaking, the Japanese experience a sense of guilt most frequently in the type of relationship where *giri* is at work and where betrayal could lead to the severing of the link. The word *sumanai*

31

serves as the most appropriate confession of the sense of guilt in such a case. Moreover, although the sense of guilt as such begins, one might say, when one has done something that one should not, the general view is that there is no admission of one's guilt unless the misdeed is accompanied by a feeling of *sumanai*. The sense of guilt summed up in the word *sumanai* naturally connects up directly with the actual act of apology. The Japanese sense of guilt, thus, shows a very clearcut structure, commencing as it does with betrayal and ending in apology; it represents, in fact, the very prototype of the sense of guilt, and Benedict's failure to see this can only be attributed to her cultural prejudice.

2

Japanese Religions

AN INTRODUCTION

By ESBEN ANDREASEN

JAPANESE RELIGIOSITY

Probably the first surprising thing that strikes a Western student when studying Japanese religions is that the average Japanese has more than one religion. According to *Japan: An International Comparison* (1990, Keizai Koho Center, Tokyo), the figures are as follows for the followers to the main religions:

Shinto	112,203,000
Buddhism	93,396,000
Christianity	1,422,000
Other religions, incl. New Religions	11,412,000
Total	218,433,000

As the population of Japan is about 120 million people this means that many Japanese adhere to two and sometimes even three religions.

If you add to this the fact that only between 25 and 35 per cent of the population claim they have a *personal* religion, the picture gets even more complex. But lack of belief in a specific religion does not mean a rejection of religious practices or of participation in religious rituals. According to surveys about 60 per cent of the Japanese turn to the gods in time of distress, more than half the

33

population believe in the existence of a 'soul' after death and about 63 per cent pay attention to lucky and unlucky days. Charms and fortune-telling are popular among about 75 per cent of the population, about 75 per cent of the homes have family altars (*kamidana* and/or *butsudan*) and over 80 per cent of the population takes part in New Year visits to Shinto shrines or Buddhist temples.

Modern Japanese are not eager to declare themselves religious when asked, but religion in Japan has always been more a matter of participation in religious rituals than a matter of holding specific beliefs. Rituals connected with religion, both private and public, are so much everyday events that very few Japanese are not involved in one way or another.

Both this diversity and practice-oriented religiosity must be understood against the backdrop of Japanese religious history.

HISTORICAL OUTLINE

1. Early Shinto

The original religious cult, before the coming of Buddhism in the 6th century A.D., is usually called 'Early Shinto', it was not, however, a coherent system of beliefs or practices. Our sources for reconstructing the religious system are the chronicles called the *Kojiki* and the *Nihon Shoki*, which outline the myths centring around the Imperial House, and the *Engishiki* which contains detailed descriptions of a number of Early Shinto prayers (*norito*) and rituals. It must, however, be emphasised that there were other cults belonging to the masses which were orally transmitted and never written down, so the term Early Shinto usually refers to the religion of the Imperial Court.

The universe we meet in the written sources has three levels: the High Plain of Heaven (*Takamagahara*) where the gods (*kami*) dwell, the world known to man, and *yomi*, a polluted nether world. The *kami* were spiritual powers or gods who could be benevolent and benefit man, but also could punish with curses when offended by pollutions of various kinds. Such offences can be reduced to two kinds: those dealing with impurity from connection with death, and those stemming from blood. Any violation of taboos would lead to the *kami's* punishment in the form of illness, fire and other accidents. There was no full-grown ethical system but the Great Purification ritual (*o-harai*) in the *Engishiki* lists a number of earthly offences to be avoided.

'*Daibatsu*' (a great image of Buddha) in the Todaiji Temple, Nara

2. Buddhism

When Buddhism was introduced, the Japanese met a totally different outlook on life which taught them to reject our world full of suffering. The Japanese, however, never absorbed the gloomy Buddhist doctrines of suffering and reincarnation for they have been more concerned with Buddhist compassion for the living and reverence for life. In particular they have concentrated on two functions of Buddhism. The first has to do with death and the pacifying of evil spirits. Early Shinto - and modern Shinto, too - feared death, but as early as the sixth century we find Buddhist requiem masses performed for the court. The second function was to offer magical spells for various benefits such as prosperity, health and peace - a function which also continues, like the death ceremonies, to be a major role of Buddhism today.

Buddhism came to Japan in a series of waves. According to *Nihon Shoki* a statue and some sutras (Buddhist texts) were sent from Korea to Japan in 552 A.D. and this marks the beginning of Japanese Buddhism which for many centuries, like Early Shinto, remained largely a religion of the nobility and upper classes. The coming of the religion was not without problems, with feuding aristocratic families either championing the new religion or supporting the old (Shinto). At first the supporters of the *kami* won out, but eventually those seeking to venerate the Buddhas overcame them.

By the late sixth century Buddhism had won the day and Prince

Shotoku's 17 article constitution of 604 A.D., with its foundations in Buddhist ethics and which set out principles for governing the country, confirms this fact.

The 17 articles also bring to light another foreign outlook on life absorbed from China, Confucianism, which will be commented on later. Buddhism flourished at the old capital of Nara in the eighth century, developing six schools of thought: Sanron, Jojitsu, Hosso, Kusha, Ritsu and Kegon. The last school, Kegon, was, like some of the others, meant to be the state religion of Japan and the Todaiji temple with its colossal Great Buddha statue was built to be its central temple. However, none of these classical schools of Nara Buddhism have a large following today.

However, the next Buddhist wave saw the growth of two sects, Tendai and Shingon, which are of importance today. They belong to the Heian (Kyoto) Period (794-1185) and were competitors, each with a mountain stronghold, Hiei-san and Koya-san (san means mountain) respectively. Tendai gave priority to the Lotus Sutra, one of the most important Mahayana Buddhist texts and probably the most important in Japan, whereas Shingon reveres two mandalas (sacred depictions of the Buddhist universe) which provide the adherents with mystic insight into Buddhist doctrines. The founder of Shingon, Kukai or Kobo Daishi, is honoured today, not only for his religious thinking, but as the great example of the prolific Heian culture. He is credited with being a master of sculpture, poetry, painting, languages (Chinese) and calligraphy.

Towards the end of the Heian Period but especially in the Kamakura Period (1185-1333), Buddhism became for the first time a truly popular religion, due to the new Amidist schools. These schools, of which Jodo and Jodo-shin are the biggest today, turned Buddhism into a religion of salvation, in which the believers, rather than helping themselves, rely on salvation through the benevolence of Amida Buddha. The world is considered evil and man helpless, and only through complete faith in Amida Buddha and by repeating the invocation, Namu Amida Buddha (Praised by Amida Buddha), can salvation occur, with Amida welcoming man into his paradise, 'The Pure Land'.

Contrary to Pure Land Buddhism, the two Zen sects that also developed in the Kamakura period emphasise self help, either through zazen (sitting meditation), as in Soto Zen, or through koan (meditational puzzles), as in Rinzai Zen. Although Zen has been called the typical Japanese development of Buddhism, it must be added that the Zen schools are by no means as large numerically as some of the other Buddhist schools in Japan.

One of these is the Nichiren sect, founded by and named after Nichiren, the intolerant reformer of Buddhism, which developed in the same period as the Zen schools. Nichiren preached a terrestrial paradise in a future Japan and for this reason he is popular to this day among nationalists. Today his brand of Buddhism has a large following, and has had many offshoots, the best known of which is the new religion called Soka Gakkai.

3. Taoism

Early Chinese influence also meant Confucianism and Taoism. Confucianism was not a religion proper at any time in Japan but has long dominated the ethics of the country. It will be discussed later in a brief section called 'Neo-Confucianism'.

Taoism did not become an independent religion either, but was absorbed into Buddhism and Shinto, especially the latter. Its influence has been on popular beliefs and superstitions concerning taboos as to time, place, and direction. Concepts of lucky and unlucky days, the evil north-easterly direction, and many other instances of popular belief are alive even in today's Japan, and these are usually considered to have derived from Taoist influences. When Chinese Taoist astrology and geomancy (the art of divination by figures and lines on the ground) came to Japan in the seventh century, an official ministry was formed to deal with such metaphysical matters.

4. Christianity

Christianity came to Japan from the Western world in three waves: in 1549 (which marks the beginning of the so-called 'Christian century'), after 1853 (when Japan was forced open by the USA), and after the Second World War. Today it seems safe to say that Christianity will not become an important religion in Japan in terms of numbers of adherents, but it has influenced the Japanese history of ideas, especially in its care for the individual and its social attitudes. One of the reasons why Christianity has not spread more rapidly is that, compared to the other religions in Japan, it has demanded of its adherents that they have no other religion than Christianity - a demand which is contrary to the inclusiveness and diversity of Japanese religiosity.

The first missionaries were Portuguese Jesuits and later Spanish Franciscans. They came not only to spread the Gospel but also to trade with Japan, and they were succeeded by the English and the Dutch, the latter becoming the only European nation whom Japan granted permission to uphold a trading station, the small island of Deshima in the harbour of Nagasaki, after Christianity was proscribed in 1639 and Japan isolated itself from the surrounding

A *Namban* screen (total 6 panels) showing Portuguese merchants and the Jesuit residence in Nagasaki. Sixteenth century.

world. In this period the position of Buddhism was strengthened, among other things by an edict which told all families to register at a Buddhist temple. Christianity was banned because Japan's rulers feared it was a vehicle through which European domination of their country would spread, as had happened in other parts of the world.

The second time Christianity came to Japan it appeared that a number of Japanese Christian families had survived the earlier persecution. They came out of hiding in the tolerant religious climate of the early Meiji Period (1868-1912), and this incident contributed to Japan lifting its ban on Christianity in 1873. But around 1890 Japan chose Shinto as the cornerstone of the new nation state and religious freedom again became an empty phrase. Still, many intellectuals converted to Christianity and at the beginning of this century, Christianity influenced the spheres of education, social legislation and labour unions in Japan. In the 1930s there were also Christian pacifists and socialists, but they were persecuted and many joined the nationalist wave. The Japanese Christian Church, as an institution, supported emperor worship and the nationalist belief in Japan as the chosen country towards the end of the Second World War (the *kokutai* philosophy).

After the War the Christian Church grew in numbers, but still it is a foreign religion in Japan and the expected growth has not come. It has, however, become somewhat fashionable to get married in a Christian church and to celebrate Christmas.

5. Neo-Confucianism

Confucianism came to Japan along with other Chinese influences in the sixth century. Prince Shotoku's 17-article Constitution is dominated by Confucian ethics and political ideology. Confucian ideals remain strong: although the Japanese are born into Shinto, get married in Shinto shrines, and are buried with Buddhist rituals, Confucian social ethics still largely govern their lives.

In Confucian thought the universe is naturally and essentially hierarchical and all men unequal. It is a fitting creed for maintaining existing relations between ruler and ruled, and in the eighteenth and nineteenth centuries a revival of Confucianism set in, known as Neo-Confucianism, coinciding with another revival, that of Shinto.

6. The Revival of Shinto

For centuries Shinto had been neglected by educated people and had become mixed up with Buddhism, but with Buddhism having the upper hand. The Shinto revival in the eighteenth century was a movement to rediscover Shinto in its ancient purity. At the same time two ideas were developed: the notion of a Japanese golden age in the past before Japan got corrupted and flooded by Chinese thought, and the belief in the superiority of the Japanese race because of the special act of divine creation related in the *Kojiki* and *Nihon Shoki* myths.

From the middle of the nineteenth century the combination of Confucian ethics and Shinto myths became a powerful force as seen in such documents of the time as the Imperial Rescript on Education (1890). Shinto was separated from Buddhism and with help from the new Meiji government, Buddhist temples were for a brief period forcibly converted into Shinto shrines or torn down.

The fatal connection between Shinto and Confucianism is well known. It had great success in the 1930s, through the *kokutai* philosophy, which preached belief in Japan as the country chosen by the Shinto gods and Japan as one body (*kokutai* = body of the country) with the Emperor as a father-figure head. However, it ended in disaster with total military defeat at the end of the Second World War, the forced renunciation of the Emperor's divinity and the instigation of real religious freedom under the new constitution.

7. The New Religions

One result of religious freedom and the separation of state and religion was the extraordinary growth of new religions so that by 1951 the number of officially registered groups had risen to 720.

Some were exposed as frauds, being merely religious 'bodies' formed to avoid paying tax. Still, the new religions filled a demand in a country in acute crisis due to the defeat, occupation by a foreign power and the collapse of State Shinto.

The new religions have turned out to be vigorous and dynamic movements. Many are messianic and build on prophecies made by founders in a state of divine revelation. Many of their founders are female, a characteristic that can be traced to the shamanesses of ancient Japan and, unlike the other religious traditions which have been male-dominated, have allowed women to play an active religious role. Some practice spiritual healing and some are mainly involved with group therapy, but in general they are active in helping people solve their problems, and their growth has been one of the most prominent features of recent Japanese religious history.

THE CHARACTERISTICS OF RELIGION IN JAPAN

A historical outline, like the preceding one, runs the risk of emphasising differences rather than similarities in order to analyse the various traditions. To give an overall view of Japanese religiosity it is necessary to describe how they fit together, and present some of the common features that occur throughout the Japanese religious world. Several such features are outlined below.

(1) The first is *mutual interaction* which means not only that the various religions intermingle but also that Japanese people and families participate in rituals from a number of religious traditions.

(2) Another feature is the *closeness between man, gods and nature*. In traditional Japanese religious thought man is not considered a 'fallen' creature, nor the ruler of nature. The notion of *kami* includes many manifestations of nature, human beings and the gods of the myths. Thus the *kami* are not considered to be in another world, but are thought to exist in nature and in the lives of men.

(3) A third characteristic is the *religious significance of the family and ancestors*. Unlike the Western world, where religion is considered to be a private matter in which the individual is the judge, religious practice in Japan is largely centred on the family as a unit. This can be traced to the clan structure of ancient society and also to Confucianism with its insistence on filial piety and hierarchical order within the family. Dead members of the family are venerated as ancestors who guard over and bring happiness and prosperity to the household.

(4) A fourth feature is *purification as a basic principle of religious life*. Sin is not a violation of divine commandments, but a state of impurity which separates one from one's fellow men and the *kami*. Sickness, wounds, childbirth and death are such instances of

Crowds pass through the torii gateway at Kyoto's Fushimi Inari Shrine

impurity. Wind, water and salt are the age-old remedies used in the rites of purification, which bring about a sense of regeneration and renewal.

(5) Fifth is the importance of *festivals (matsuri) as major religious celebrations*. There are no weekly religious services in Japanese religions, but there are numerous special festival days throughout the year at shrines and temples, such as spring and harvest *matsuri*, New Year, *bon* festivals for the dead, in addition to a number of rites of passage for the individual.

(6) This division into seasons also explains the next feature: *religion is practised daily*. Religion was not separate from everyday life in traditional Japan: for example, every stage in rice production required rituals and other religious activities. The close relationship of religion and daily life still continues, as can be seen by the presence in most households of the *kamidana* (Shinto altar) and *butsudan* (Buddhist altar for the ancestors) at which people pray regularly.

(7) Finally, there has long been *a close relationship between religion and state*. From the days of Prince Shotoku and even before when Japan consisted of clans, the head of the state or the clan was also the leading religious officiant, at least symbolically. The *Kojiki* and *Nihon Shoki* myths emphasised this link between the world of the gods and Japan through the idea that the *kami* created Japan as a sacred land to be ruled by the emperor who was a descendant of the sun goddess, Amaterasu. Support of the state by religion continued until the end of the Second World War and was upheld

by most religious groups, not only Shinto, but also Buddhist and Christian. Nowadays state and religion are legally separate under the terms of the 1946 Constitution.

In all of the seven features it is safe to say that there are strong influences from early Shinto, and that these remain the underlying basis of much of Japanese religiosity.

THE JAPANESE MELTING POT

In order to feel at home in our life on earth, man seeks answers to a number of questions, the sum of which make up a philosophy of life. These include questions concerning good and evil (ethics), true and false (science), being and not-being (metaphysics), and ugly and beautiful (aesthetics). In such a simplified ordering it can be said that for a modern Japanese ethics belongs to Confucianism, science to Western materialistic science, metaphysics to Buddhism and aesthetics to Shinto.

It is said that Prince Shotoku compared the religions of Japan to a cooking pot on a tripod where the three legs are Confucianism, Shinto and Buddhism. Today, to this picture must be added the scientific outlook on life and symbolically this dimension may well fit into the image as the lid of the pot. The point is that the pot is a melting pot where all the ingredients can be mixed. Many historians of religion compare Japan to a laboratory of religions, and this in essence uses the same image.

What the three ingredients - Shinto, Confucianism and Buddhism - stand for has been set out above in the 'Historical Outline'. Western science and technology need not be explained to a Western audience. What we now need to understand is the thesis that no religion or ideology precludes or counteracts the others and that nothing is eliminated; rather all function together and supplement each other,

Take Buddhism and Shinto and the well-known division of labour between them. Shinto focuses on rituals of fertility, purification, rites of passage and growth, and Buddhism concerns itself with illness, death, enlightenment and education. Together they form a whole series of rituals which accompany the individual from birth (Shinto) to death (Buddhism). The Japanese mentality which could combine these two religions into one framework also explains how the *kami* and Buddhist deities could work together. Buddhist gods were accepted as new *kami* in Shinto, and Shinto gods were interpreted as Bodhisattvas (enlightened beings) in Buddhism. Even today the Japanese use one word, *shinbutsu* to refer to *kami* and Buddhas together.

There is the example, too, of Confucianism and modern

technology. When Western technology came to Japan there was no resistance to the change in life patterns this caused. The work ethic needed to boost production could be found in Confucianism and its weight on duty, industry and harmony between ruler and ruled. The Confucian ethics they learned at home and at school helped make Japan's labour force ideal workers in the new factories. The slogan from the early Meiji Period, 'Western science and Eastern ethics' proved a valid and viable union of the two ways.

The new religions are often products of the union between aspects of Buddhism, Shinto, Confucianism and sometimes even Christianity. Many new religions take elements of their doctrines, practices, cosmologies and rituals from all of these religions and fuse them into a coherent whole.

One final example of the inclusiveness of Japanese religiosity is the way Christianity came to be accepted in Japan in its early successful decades around the second half of the sixteenth century. The Japanese were able to fit Christianity into the religions of Japan by understanding the new faith as yet another wave of Buddhism from the Asian continent. Especially the messengers of salvation in Buddhism, the bodhisattvas, were of use in this respect, and the Virgin Mary was identified with the female bodhisattva of mercy called Kannon. If Christianity had not refused to participate in such a blend, it would undoubtedly have been assimilated into the Japanese religious melting pot rather than being banned.

*Note: The introductory chapter is indebted to other studies of Japanese religions. The first part with sociological data builds on Jan Swyngedouw: 'Religion in Contemporary Japanese Society', *The East*, Vol. 22, No. 3 (May 1986). The 'Brief Historical Outline', likewise, on Carmen Blacker: 'The Religions of Japan', *Historia Religionum*, Vol. II (Leiden 1971). The 'Characteristics' uses H. Byron Earhart's classifications in some of his books, and his article about religion in *Encyclopedia of Japan*, (Kodansha 1983). Finally, 'The Japanese Melting Pot' is inspired by a lecture given in October 1986 by Olof G. Lidin, Copenhagen University, whose *Japans religioner*, (Politiken 1985) - unfortunately not translated from the Danish into other languages - is one of the best book-length introductions to our knowledge.

3

Folk Religion

By IAN READER

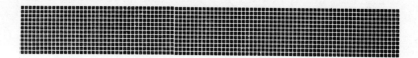

In the previous chapter we encountered the various religious traditions found in Japan, along with a brief historical outline of their
development and common characteristics. Probably the most
striking of these characteristics were that the various religious
traditions tended to work together rather than conflict with each
other, and that the Japanese usually belong to more than one religion
and incorporate different religious traditions into their lives.

Underlying this sense of multiple belonging and the close
relationship of daily life and religion is the strong and enduring
popular Japanese folk religious tradition which will be examined in
this chapter.

Folk religion in general is unstructured, with no set doctrines or
organisation. Instead it consists of various practices, commonly-held
beliefs, assumptions and customs that can be expressed through
various different religious channels depending on the circumstances.
In other words, the folk religious tradition is closely related to the
everyday lives of the people, to their cultural background and shared
views of life and the world around them.

Because of this close connection with the everyday lives and
attitudes of the people the folk religious tradition could be described
as popular religion and as the everyday religion of the people. As
such it is likely to make its influence felt on any religion that grows
in that society. This is certainly the case in Japan where Shinto,
Buddhism and the new religions have been strongly influenced by
folk and popular religious practices. Indeed much of what goes on

at Shinto shrines and Buddhist temples, as well as many of the activities in the household that are associated with Shinto and Buddhism, can be seen as expressions of this popular folk religiosity.

In this chapter we will look at a number of aspects of folk religion in Japan and at areas in which it plays a part in the lives of Japanese people. In particular we will focus on five main themes in Japanese folk religion: (1) prayers, charms and popular deities, (2) oracles and divination, (3) life-cycles, calendrical rites and festivals, (4) the ancestors and religion in the home, and (5) unhappy spirits of the dead, misfortune and exorcism.

The Thousand-Armed Statue of Kannon, Sanjusangendo Temple, Kyoto

1. PRAYERS, CHARMS AND POPULAR DEITIES

One of the basic elements of folk religion is that it is human centred and concerned with life in the present, dealing especially with practical issues in people's lives, and with seeking to bring them good fortune and to deal directly with misfortunes. People do not have to hold to any previously determined beliefs before participating in folk and popular religious practices: in fact, one of the main motivations for doing so is because of particular circumstances affecting them at a specific time.

At the beginning of Chapter Two it was mentioned that 60 per cent of the Japanese turn to the gods in times of distress, and this can be seen as a basic expression of the popular folk religious tradition. The deities in the Japanese religious traditions (whether the *kami* or gods of Shinto or the various Buddhas and deities of Buddhism) are there, in the popular view, for the benefit of humans, to be called on when someone is in need, to help and support them.

A good example of this can be found in the behaviour of Japanese students before their examinations. On their way through the demanding Japanese education system students have to undertake several extremely crucial examinations. Passing them will get them into a good school or university, and this in itself can open the way to a good career afterwards. Failure, on the other hand, may mean entering a poor school, failing to gain a college place and hence having trouble in the job market afterwards.

Understandably, then, students find themselves under great pressure, especially in January and February, when the national school and university entrance examinations take place. It is at these times in particular that large numbers of students visit popular shrines and temples to pray to the gods and Buddhas and ask for their support. It does not matter that at other times they might never go to such places, or that they would normally consider themselves to be not religious: when they are faced with problems, and when the situation demands it, they will turn to the gods and pray for success.

Japanese people pray to the gods and Buddhas not only in times of trouble but also to gain their protection when embarking on new ventures, to enlist their help in carrying out their daily activities and to ensure they have a prosperous life. There is very little differentiation here between the Shinto gods and the Buddhist deities: at the folk and popular religious level what matters to people are the benefits that these entities can bestow on them or can help them attain. Popular deities are invoked not because of the religious tradition they belong to but for what they can provide in terms of emotional support and other benefits.

A *kake-botoke* ('hanging Buddha') plaque. Kamakura period, 13th century

The Daruma doll is one of the most popular talismans to be found in Japan; it is a symbol of good luck signifying the determination to complete a task successfully. Here the second 'eye' (task completed) is being painted in.

Indeed it is common to pray to figures of worship from different traditions depending on circumstances. A young single woman may, for example, visit a Shinto shrine dedicated to Tenjin, a god associated with education, for help when taking her university examinations. Later she may visit a different shrine to ask a god popularly associated with love and marriage to pray for help in finding a husband: when married and pregnant she may go to a temple and ask Kannon, the Buddhist figure of mercy who is associated also with childbirth, to ensure she has a safe and easy delivery and a healthy baby.

Her husband may follow similar patterns in accord with his needs and life patterns. If, for example, he has bought a car he might take it to a Buddhist temple and have it blessed or purchase a protective amulet for traffic safety, which he will place in the car. He might then pray to a god such as Inari, the fox deity associated with business prosperity, when he is hoping for promotion in his company or, if he runs his own business, might go to a shrine associated with Ebisu, a deity of commerce and good fortune, to seek his help.

When praying to the gods Japanese people often acquire various religious charms, talismans from shrines and temples, and these are a further aspect of folk religion. Such charms symbolise the power and presence of the deities and are usually carried on the person or placed in the home. They also reflect the nature of the prayers that

47

people direct to the *kami* and Buddhas, and cover virtually every area of human enterprise and need one could imagine. One can find charms for safe birth, for educational success, for traffic safety, family happiness, business prosperity, a happy love life, and much more besides.

The most common sorts of charm are called *o-mamori* and are small colourful brocade bags on which the name of the shrine or temple and the benefit desired are written. Inside the bag is usually a piece of paper or wood inscribed with a prayer. Large numbers of Japanese carry *o-mamori* and other such charms at some time or other: surveys have shown that over 70 per cent of Japanese of all ages use them either sometimes or often.

Fox statue at Inari shrine

O-mamori

Jizo looking after the souls of dead babies

This does not mean that the Japanese believe that an amulet or lucky charm will make them pass an examination, or that a prayer to a god will prevent accidents or cause their company to be successful. To a great degree charms and amulets, as with praying to the gods, are emotional means of support and reassurance. They remind one that one is not alone in one's endeavour, while also serving as a reminder of a task in hand: an amulet for educational success reminds the student of the need to study hard and offers support in this, while one for traffic safety hanging in the car reminds the driver of the importance of driving carefully so as to avoid accidents.

Praying to the gods and buying charms and amulets also affirms an underlying notion that still finds much support among Japanese of all ages, which considers that man does not live on this earth in a vacuum, but in relationship with all around him.

It is quite common, too, for people to become devoted followers and worshippers of the popular deities that are invoked in times of trouble or in pursuit of practical benefits. The Buddhist figures Jizo and Kannon are especially popular in this respect. Jizo is a bald-headed figure who protects travellers, children (including those who die very young) and anyone who is in an unsettled state.

Statues of Jizo are often found on mountain passes, where he protects travellers and those far from home. In Buddhist folk tales he often rescues the souls of children from the hells into which they have inadvertently fallen, and looks after the souls of babies who die in the womb. It is common to see statues of Jizo dressed up with bibs and hats: these are put there by devotees, the hats to keep him warm and the bibs (which usually have the name of a child on them) to remind him of whom to save.

Kannon is perhaps even more popular. This female Buddha figure is the embodiment of compassion and is greatly loved for her vow to rescue anyone in distress. People pray to Kannon for all manner of things, but she has a special following among women who seek her support when they are pregnant, and among old people who ask her to give them a peaceful old age free of the problem of senility. There are also several pilgrimages in Japan dedicated to Kannon that attract thousands of pilgrims every year.

2. ORACLES AND DIVINATION

Another area of folk religion that continues to influence the lives and practices of many Japanese is a concern with divination and with lucky and unlucky days and directions. Many of these ideas originated from Taoism but have since become part of the general Japanese folk religious culture. Fortune-telling and divination played a major part in Japanese life in earlier ages, with oracles consulted before undertaking new projects, and with diviners consulted about the correct day to start an enterprise or the best possible position in which to build a house.

Many Japanese still take note of these things. Before building a new house, or before moving elsewhere it is common to consult a diviner to make sure that the proposed orientation of the house will not be unlucky. Certain directions (in particular the north-east, known as the *kimon* or 'devil's gate') are especially unlucky and are avoided. Similar consultations take place when building a grave, for siting it facing an unlucky direction is believed to cause distress to the spirits of the dead and prevent them reaching a state of peace.

Over 60 per cent of the Japanese state that they take notice of lucky and unlucky days: although the Japanese use the seven-day week many people still remain aware of the traditional six-day cycle in which each day is classified in varying degrees of good and bad luck. The luckiest day in this cycle is known as the *taian* ('great peace') and is the best day for marriages and starting projects, while the unluckiest days such as the *butsumetsu* ('death of the Buddha') clearly are not. In fact it costs more money to hire wedding halls and hold receptions on *taian* than other days because the demand is higher than at other times, while the cheapest times for marriage are *butsumetsu* - although few would consider marrying on a day associated with death. Large numbers of Japanese also consult an almanac or a diviner for the most auspicious day for a wedding, taking into account also the zodiacal signs and the horoscopes of those getting married.

The concept of lucky and unlucky times extends to different ages and years as well. Certain ages are regarded as especially lucky (60 in particular), while others are especially unlucky. People take particular note of these unlucky years, the main ones of which are the age of 42 for men and 33 for women, and may visit a shrine or temple to receive a special ritual purification and seek the gods' protection.

Schoolchildren reading *o-mikuji* at Yasaka shrine, Kyoto. (See special frame for tying *o-mikuji*)

This interest in prediction and divination extends to fortune-telling as well. Slips of paper called *o-mikuji* (divination slips or oracle lots) that predict one's fortune can be acquired at shrines and temples alike on payment of a small fee (see Reading No. 7 for the translation of a typical divination slip). Horoscopes, almanacs and palm-reading all remain popular as well.

This does not mean that the Japanese believe implicitly in divination and in lucky days, or that they are a superstitious people ruled by fortune-telling and oracles. Divination practices such as the acquisition of *o-mikuji* are also often done in a light-hearted manner, in the same way that people read their horoscopes in the West, and reflect an interest in speculating about what the future might hold rather than a belief in the overriding power of fate. Many people also simply consider it best to play safe and take precautions against the possibility of bad luck, especially when by so conforming to customs and cultural traditions they will please those around them such as their parents, grandparents and ancestors. For all these reasons divination, oracles and ideas of lucky and unlucky days, years and directions continue to be an active element of Japanese folk religion today.

3. LIFE-CYCLES, CALENDRICAL RITES AND FESTIVALS

Another aspect of Japanese folk religion and popular religious practice is connected with the yearly calendar and with the life-cycle of individuals and their families. Different times of the year in earlier, pre-industrial Japanese society were occasions for special rituals and festivals connected to the gods, Buddhas and ancestors, and many of these continue to be important in modern times, among urban and rural Japanese alike.

Different times in the life-cycle of the individual, too, are occasions for religious rituals and festivals, and these remain part of the social and cultural aspects of religion that most Japanese participate in.

The Japanese say that they are born Shinto and die Buddhist, and this indicates how the two great religious traditions in Japan each play a role in the life-cycles of individuals. It is customary to take new-born babies to a Shinto shrine soon after birth to present them to the gods and receive their blessing for a good and prosperous life. Buddhism is the vehicle through which death is handled: most Japanese have Buddhist funerals and their families take part in a series of Buddhist rites that are believed to guide the spirit of the dead to the world of the ancestors.

In terms of yearly events with religious undertones and meanings the largest and most prominent are the New Year festival in January and the *bon* festival, which occurs in August in most parts of Japan. New Year is a happy and joyous time of new beginnings that symbolise renewal and regeneration. It is a time for family gatherings and for a variety of activities such as communal meals and cleaning the house so as to symbolically sweep aside the dust of the past and start anew.

At this time most Japanese visit Shinto shrines to greet the gods anew and to pray to them for good luck in the coming year. Many also visit Buddhist temples as well, and in all it is estimated that over 80 million people, or three-quarters of the population, will make a visit to a shrine or temple in the first three days of the year. When doing so they usually not only pray for good luck but also get an *o-mikuji* to predict their fate in the coming year and buy a lucky charm or two as well.

Bon is the festival of the dead, when the spirits of the ancestors are believed to return to earth for a short period in the summer to be with their living kin. Although *bon* is connected with death it is not so much a sombre affair as a celebration of the continuation of life. The Japanese consider that their ancestors do not leave them at death but continue to be part of the household, looking after and overseeing the fortunes of the living members of their families.

At *bon* the ancestors are believed to return to earth, to their native villages, to be with their kin. At this time most Japanese return to their family homes for the festival, visit their family graves to make offerings to the ancestors and go to their local Buddhist temples to perform memorial services for them.

As well as the *bon* festival there are other times in the year when memorial services are done for the dead, notably at the festival of *higan* that occurs at the spring and autumn equinoxes in March and September. At this time families also gather to visit the family grave, clean it and make offerings to their ancestors. Recent statistics show that close to 90 per cent of the Japanese take part in these festivals centred on their ancestors and follow the practice known as *haka mairi*, visiting the graves of the ancestors.

Besides these two events there are numerous other festive occasions throughout the year that large numbers of Japanese people take part in. Many of these have their roots in the agricultural cycle and are found in rituals connected with planting and the harvest. This demonstrates that although Japan is now a modern industrial nation, it still retains a strong connection to its old rural traditions, and that its origins as an agricultural, and especially as a rice farming, society still manifest themselves today.

Shichi-go-san (literally seven-five-three) is celebrated on 15 November when girls aged three or seven and boys aged five or seven are taken to the local shrine to pray for good health.

In February there is the *setsubun* festival which traditionally greeted the coming of spring: at this time it is common to visit shrines and temples to pray for good luck and for the eradication of evil, while March and April are times when rice-planting festivals occur at Shinto shrines throughout Japan.

In the heat of summer there are large numbers of evening festivals, while September and October are the occasions for festivals celebrating the harvest - even in areas where little or no farming now takes place! On 15 November the *shichigosan* (7-5-3) festival takes place. This is a children's festival in which girls of three and seven and boys of five are dressed in special clothes (usually a kimono) and taken to a shrine by their parents, to receive a blessing from the gods.

These are only some of the many festivals that take place in Japan. Besides these major affairs that are celebrated all over the country there are hundreds of smaller local ones, perhaps commemorating a local event or a religious story. Festivals are generally noisy and lively affairs combining entertainment and religious actions. Usually centred on Shinto shrines they celebrate the joy of life and have, as one of their central motifs, the theme of paying thanks to the gods for the good things they have bestowed on the living, while also performing homage to them so that they may give further benefits in the future. Shrine courtyards, and the streets before shrines, are usually turned into open-air markets at festivals, with stalls selling food, drink, toys, trinkets and souvenirs. They are occasions for letting off steam and enjoying oneself and it is common for large amounts of saké (rice wine) to be consumed at them. In attending festivals people have the chance to have a good time with their friends and families, to relax, eat, drink - and pray.

4. THE ANCESTORS AND RELIGION IN THE HOME

All the events mentioned in the previous section combine social, cultural, festive and religious themes at once and are good examples of how religion still remains very much an affair concerned with the everyday lives of Japanese people. A further example of this close link between everyday life and religion can be found in the typical Japanese home itself, which has a religious symbolism of its own.

Before any house or other building is put up in Japan it is customary to have a Shinto ceremony known as *jichinsai* or ground breaking ceremony in which the local gods are asked to bestow their blessings and protection on the house. Many households and buildings have a *kamidana*, a small Shinto altar in which the protective gods (*kami*) of the house are enshrined and before which ritual offerings (usually food, water and flowers) are made regularly. *Kamidana* are seen not just in houses but in shops, stores and even business offices as well. ₁

Perhaps even more important for the household is the *butsudan*, the family Buddhist altar that enshrines the ancestors of the family.

Family graves

Family shrine - *butsudan*. Photo: Takadate Chieko

Over 60 per cent of Japanese households have a *butsudan*: many of the rest do not simply because no-one in the family has yet died and become an ancestor. *Butsudan* are cabinets usually made of lacquered wood which contain various Buddhist ornaments such as candles, small Buddhist statues and an incense holder, as well as mortuary tablets that represent the spirit of the ancestor and to which prayers are addressed and offerings made.

In old traditional houses one often finds a special room that is set aside for the altar. In the more cramped modern apartments that today's urban Japanese live in there is less space for the altars and they tend to be smaller and more compact than in former times, although usually placed in an elevated position to denote their importance.

The Japanese believe that each person has a soul or spirit that continues to exist after death and that continues to be attached to its family and surroundings. When a person dies their family and close kin will go into mourning for a period of 49 days, during which time it is believed that the spirit of the dead person remains close to the family home.

In this 49-day period a series of Buddhist rituals take place, in which both the Buddhist priest of the local temple and the family themselves take part. Through these rites it is believed that the spirit is purified of all the unhappiness and dangers associated with death, and will be transformed into an ancestor, a contented spirit in the world of the dead who looks over and benevolently guards its living kin. Besides the funeral there is a rite that bestows on the dead spirit a *kaimyo*, a special posthumous name that gives the spirit a new identity fitting to its new state as belonging not to this world but to the world of the dead and of the ancestors.

At the end of 49 days, after all the rituals have been performed, the dead spirit is believed to have entered the world of the ancestors from where it will oversee the lives of the living. At this time a mortuary tablet, usually around six inches high and two inches wide, covered in black lacquer, is made to represent the spirit of the ancestor. The ancestor's new name, the *kaimyo*, is carved on this tablet, which is then placed in the *butsudan*.

Regular memorial services are performed before the *butsudan* as well as at the grave, especially on anniversaries of the death, and it is common for families to summon a Buddhist priest to do this. It is traditional to continue performing these services until the 33rd or 50th anniversary of death.

Often, too, family members will make daily acts of worship at the *butsudan* in their home, and may even 'talk' to the ancestors there, relaying pieces of family news to them. The ancestors are in these ways seen as an integral part of the family and household: having given life to the family they represent a sense of continuity, of tradition and peaceful prosperity. They help reinforce the strong sense of social responsibility to the family name that is found in Japan and act as a reminder to the living of their obligations to this heritage. Sometimes, indeed, the ancestors are called into action by parents seeking to keep their children well behaved: children are not only told to act well for the sake of the ancestors but may be made to apologise to the ancestors at the *butsudan* when they have been naughty.

The ancestors remain a very major and central element in the overall religious life of Japan. There are very few Japanese - even those who profess to have no religious beliefs at all - who do not take part in some of the various rites connected with the ancestors. In fact it appears that the numbers of people taking part in such activities connected with the ancestors as the *bon* festival, praying at the *butsudan* and visiting the grave at special times are going up in contemporary Japan. This demonstrates the continuing importance of the ancestors to Japanese society in general and to the family in particular.

The family as a social unit that includes not just the present but past and future generations is one of the most important institutions in Japan, playing a key role in the continuing stability of Japanese society. The ancestors are an essential element in providing the family, and society, with this sense of balance and continuity. This is true even in contemporary Japan where, for all the changes brought about by urbanisation, modernisation and internationalisation, the ancestors still provide many Japanese with a sense of emotional warmth, comfort and continuity that acts as a counterweight to the vast changes that are going on around them.

5. UNHAPPY SPIRITS OF THE DEAD, MISFORTUNE AND EXORCISM

Although it is customarily believed in Japan that when someone dies they will become an ancestor who looks benevolently over the living, there remains, at the folk level, an underlying fear concerning the spirits of the dead. As we shall see in the next chapter (see Reading No. 9), the fear of death and of the dangers that may come from the spirits of the dead are expressed strongly in Shinto myths. They exist, too, in the folk religious world with the idea that the spirits of those who die sudden, premature or violent deaths and of those for whom no memorial services and rituals have been performed after death will continue to exist in a relationship with this world, but in an unhappy and angry way.

There are many stories in Japanese folklore and from the past of malevolent spirits causing distress to the living, by possessing them and causing illnesses, or by creating havoc in some way in the environment. To counteract the threats posed by malevolent spirits there were large numbers of spiritual specialists and diviners who were believed to be able to contact the spirits of the dead, ascertain why they were angry and causing problems and, if necessary, to exorcise spirits from those whom they possessed. It was common, if someone became sick or suffered misfortunes, for them to consult diviners to determine the reasons for their problems.

Even in contemporary Japan these fears continue to have some influence. While virtually all Japanese go to medical practitioners when they become ill, many also follow this up with a visit to a diviner of some sort to ascertain whether there is a spiritual reason as well for the illness. There are still large numbers of diviners and spirit mediums who ply their trade in Japan today, the best known of whom are called *itako*. These are blind females who live in northern Japan and who gather at Mount Osore, a volcanic area at the very northern tip of the main island of Honshu, in a four-day festival every summer. Every year at this time thousands of Japanese of all ages flock to Mount Osore to consult the *itako*, either to seek information on why they are having problems or for help in contacting a dead relative.

The *itako*, when asked to contact a spirit of the dead or to answer a problem, begin by chanting prayers and by banging on a drum, a performance which sends them into a trance in which they can 'speak' to the dead spirit and relay its messages to the living. Often the message will inform the living that the spirit is unhappy for some reason, perhaps because its living descendant is not making enough offerings at the grave or *butsudan*, or because the ancestor is unhappy with the conduct of the living. Besides the injunction to perform more offerings the living person is often told to reform themselves in some way in order to please the spirit of the dead.

Similar processes take place in the new religions, which frequently display many aspects of folk religious belief in their activities. Large numbers of those who join new religions are motivated to do so by problems in their personal lives, and one major role that the new religions play is in helping such people to confront their problems. Frequently these explanations revolve around the role of unhappy ancestors and malevolent spirits of the dead, and, in order to make themselves better, the person is told to perform religious services that will make the spirits happy so that they will cease to cause problems. Some new religions, echoing ideas found in traditional folk religion, say illnesses or problems can come about because an unhappy or angry spirit has taken up residence in the mind of the person involved. In such cases the religion may use special techniques for exorcising these spirits and purifying the afflicted person of these bad influences.

We will deal further with these themes in Chapter Six, which centres on the new religions, and in Reading No. 42 in particular, which highlights the ideas of one new religion, Mahikari, on this matter. The numbers of people that visit the *itako* of Mount Osore and, indeed, the many diviners that make their living in Japan's cities, along with the importance given to the role of spirits in the teachings of many new religions do show that Japanese folk religious ideas about the spirits of the dead continue to be relevant and to influence many Japanese even in this modern age. This is a further indication of how the Japanese folk religious tradition remains alive and plays an active part in the lives of Japanese people, and how its influences can be found within the other religious traditions to be found in Japan.

READINGS

This chapter has looked at the main aspects of the world of Japanese folk religion today. Since many of these themes have permeated into all the other Japanese religious traditions we will encounter them again in the readings in subsequent chapters that focus on these different religions. To conclude this chapter we have selected three short readings, each of which illustrates points made earlier. Reading No. 6 is a translation of an *o-mikuji* (oracle or divination slip) of the type commonly found at temples and shrines, in this case from a Buddhist temple. It promises much in the way of good luck, although it should be added that not all *o-mikuji* do so: some warn of potential misfortunes and warn the recipients to be on their guard.

Readings 7 and 8 focus on popular figures of worship and the benevolences they bestow. No. 7 is a typical folk tale in which someone is rewarded for praying earnestly to Kannon, while No. 8 introduces the annual Jizo *bon* festival which is especially popular with children. Because Jizo looks after the souls of children he has his own special *bon* festival separate from, and just after, the main August *bon* festival. These two readings on Kannon and Jizo also show the use of cartoons in transmitting religious teachings and stories, and this is another aspect of Japanese folk religion and also of Japanese popular culture in general, for cartoons (*manga*) are widely used as means of putting across messages and for educational purposes.

Purificatory straw circle at a Shinto shrine

Reading No. 6

Oracle from Kannon in the Reizan temple

Great Happiness:

'To begin with you seem to have difficulties getting your wishes fulfilled, but in the end they will be. Be correct and honest in everything.

Lucky direction: west.

Your initiatives will succeed.

Celebrate your anniversaries confidently. Wait until the autumn before entering into personal relationships/marriage.

You will embark on a wonderful journey.

The guest you expect will not turn up in the spring or the summer.

You will hardly lose anything. If it should happen you can get it back through hard labour.

In business you will have good luck and success.

You will win your lawsuits, by and large.

Your delivery will be easy.

Your illness may look serious but will be cured. Even though you are uncertain about the diagnosis during the illness, everything will be fine. Follow the advice of your doctor and you will get well again.

If you fish you will get a good catch. Try soon!'

Reading No. 7
The straw millionaire

From a cartoon about Kannon, 1984

(The story begins in the Kannon temple, Hase, near Nara. The series of pictures must be read from right to left).
In **(2)** the main character of the cartoon, a boy, says, 'Dear Kannon. Be kind to me and give me the good luck I deserve'. **(3)** 'He prays every day. For seven days and for 14 days'.

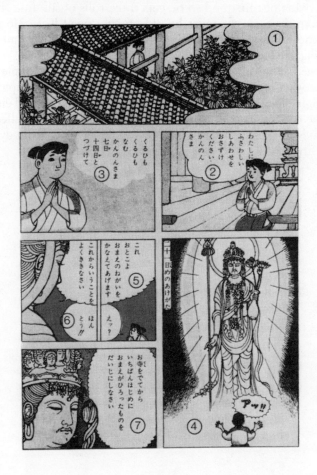

(4) 'On the 21st day: "Oh--"
(5) and **(6)** 'Listen! Your wish shall come true!' 'Pardon...?' 'Listen carefully!' 'Yes, I promise!'
(7) 'Take good care of the first thing you find after you have left the temple!'

On the following pages of the cartoon our main character walks out of the temple, grateful. And he says, 'Indeed, things begin to prosper for me after I have visited the temple'.

He sees the beautiful peonies of the temple, but suddenly he stumbles down the steps and finds - a straw. 'Oh, what have I found! A straw! I'll throw it away!' But Kannon had told him, 'Take good care of the first thing you find'. So he resolves, 'I must take good care of this piece of straw'.

He walks on and catches a gadfly which he exchanges for three mandarins from a rich man's son. His mandarins rescue a woman from dying of thirst and so he gets three rolls of silk from her.

'From then on whatever he did brought good luck. He worked diligently and got a fine harvest of rice. His store became bigger and bigger. He also got a good wife'.

Together with his wife he again visits the Hase temple which teems with beautiful flowers. 'Kannon in the Hase temple is the Kannon of Good Fortune. It deserves its name: the Flower Temple!'

The cartoon ends this way: 'By and by the boy was called "The Straw Millionaire" because he became richer than anybody would have thought - just because he picked up a straw.'

Reading No. 8
Jizo *bon*: a cartoon about Jizo

'In Japan the month of August is called *bon tsuki*, i.e. the month (*tsuki*) in which the *bon* festival is held.

Every year, 24 July or 24 August are Jizo *bon*.

The children in the town give flowers to Ojizo-sama (the stone figure) and give vegetables and fruit which can be cultivated.

Ojizo-sama is a bodhisattva (compassionate Buddha figure) with growing power, so Ojizo-sama is like the fertile soil where many things such as crops can grow.

Ojizo-sama is always together with human beings and he understands our suffering and sorrow and cares for the children.

The whole family will celebrate Ojizo-sama at Jizo *bon* on 24 July or 24 August - and thank him.

It is a very solemn occasion because parents and children pray together, and in this way the children learn to pray.'

4

Shinto

By IAN READER

Shinto is often described as Japan's national religion for it is an explicitly *Japanese* religion concerned with the Japanese people and the environment and world in which they live. The *kami*, the gods of Shinto, occur in the Japanese world, and the myths and legends of Shinto concern the creation and beginnings of the Japanese world and of the land of Japan and its people. Thus it is a religion focused on Japanese unity and community, and with the Japanese people and *their* existence in this world. It is for such reasons in particular that virtually all Japanese (see the statistics in Chapter One) are counted as belonging to Shinto: in many senses Shinto and being Japanese are synonymous.

Some of the popular and folk aspects of Shinto have been dealt with in the previous chapter, such as the presence in many households of the *kamidana* or Shinto altar, the role of the gods in bestowing benefits on the living, and the popularity of festivals. At local levels, too, Shinto has always been connected to fertility, production and the maintenance of the community.

In rural Japan the local Shinto shrine traditionally was a focal point of the community, enshrining a protective *kami* who guarded over the local area and its inhabitants, and to whom the community prayed for good harvests and for help in ensuring continued fertility and production. Shrines and their *kami* were also the focus and location of celebrations, with festivals (*matsuri*) at the harvest season and other times of year.

Such aspects of Shinto continue today as well: festivals are highly

Shinto rice-planting ceremony in central Japan

popular in contemporary Japan, while rice-planting and other agricultural rites still take place at Shinto shrines throughout the country. Furthermore, the role of the Shinto *kami* as guardians of fertility and production has been taken up also by contemporary Japanese companies and business firms, many of which patronise Shinto shrines or have small shrines built on their premises enshrining *kami* adopted as company guardians.

Shinto has another and more controversial side as well, connected to Japanese nationalism, political control and the relationship between religion and politics. The Japanese myths dealing with the relationship between the Japanese people and their *kami* focus in particular on the descent of the Japanese Imperial family from the *kami* and especially of the Emperor coming directly from Amaterasu, the powerful Sun Goddess. This myth confers a special status on the Emperor, which has at times in Japanese history been interpreted as meaning that the Emperor himself was a living deity (*ikigami*).

From the latter part of the nineteenth century until the end of the war in 1945 this was the prevailing ethic in Japan, and the Emperor, although politically weak, was portrayed as a divine unifying symbol of Japan. In 1946, after the defeat of Japan and the nationalistic government that upheld these views, Emperor Hirohito publicly renounced the notion of his own divinity, while the official links between Shinto and the Japanese state were broken.

Above: Garden of Sambo-in, Kyoto, in the grounds of Omote Shoin temple dating back to the Heian period (794-1102). It is known as one of the finest landscape gardens in Japan.
Below: Wearing traditional costumes of the Muromachi period (1336-1573), female rice planters take part in the rice-planting ceremony 'Otaue' in the precinct of Sumiyoshi Taisha Shrine, Osaka, held annually (14 June) to pray for a good harvest

However, there still remains a close link between Shinto, because it is a religion that is not concerned with other peoples but is centred wholly on Japan and Japanese identity and prosperity, and Japanese nationalism. There are some Japanese (largely of the older generation) who still consider the Emperor to be divine, and who would like to reaffirm the notion of the Japanese as a special, chosen race existing in an unique relationship with their gods.

In conflict with them are many others, ranging from Japanese Christians to members of civil liberties' and left-wing organisations, who strongly and vocally oppose any connection between the state and Shinto. Shinto thus, at national levels, remains a constant source of controversy and provokes many discussions, many of which will be taken up in Chapter Seven which deals with the question of religion and the state in Japan.

Shinto thus incorporates many diverse themes, from popular and folk-oriented elements to nationalistic and political ones. At the same time, it contains many of the elements normally associated with other religions, and it is such themes that form the basis of the readings in this chapter.

Shinto has its own sacred myths that outline, on a metaphorical level, basic underlying concepts and views of life and the world and of man's position in it. It has its special spiritual figures of worship, the *kami*, and its sacred places and centres of worship, as well as various rituals and prayers, through which to communicate with and relate to them. It is through such elements that Shinto derives its special religious nature at all levels, from the local, community and individual levels to the national ones.

AN OUTLINE OF THE READINGS

The first reading (No. 9) is taken from the *Kojiki*, one of two texts (the other is the *Nihongi*) written in the early eighth century which set down Japanese creation myths expressing many basic religious themes prevalent within Shinto. The texts are long and written in an ancient style, and they contain long lists of complex names of Japanese *kami*. All of this makes them rather difficult to read even in translation and so, for the sake of easier reading, we have selected a few short sections from the text, and have interspersed them with short linking sections summarising the passages left out. Because, also, we encounter in the *Kojiki* many themes that are basic to Shinto and to Japanese religiosity we have drawn attention to the major themes within the texts as they occur.

The second reading (No. 10) comes from Daniel Holtom's book on Shinto, written in 1938, and provides an explanation and discussion of the nature of the Shinto gods, the *kami*. The concept of *kami* is at once one of the most important and most difficult elements to grasp in the whole realm of the Japanese religious world, and Holtom's discussion provides us with a clear overview of the idea of what a *kami* is.

Readings No. 11 and No. 12 focus on the great shrines of Ise, the holiest shrines in Shinto, which are national centres of worship closely related to the Imperial family because they enshrine Amaterasu, the Sun Goddess. The shrines are rebuilt every 20 years in a pristine Japanese style dating to the seventh century: the rebuilding serves as a symbol of regeneration and renewal, and provides a link with Japan's past at the same time. Svend Hvass's description (No. 11) of the shrine, its aesthetic nature and its rebuilding, is followed by a reverent description (No. 12) of the pilgrimage made by a fourteenth-century Buddhist monk, which shows the extent to which different religious traditions could operate within one Japanese life: although a Buddhist monk, Saka clearly is struck with reverence at this great Shinto shrine.

The fifth reading (No. 13) in this section describes a Shinto shrine and its layout, using the example of the Meiji shrine in Tokyo. This reading also outlines how one should behave and pray at shrines. The final readings (Nos. 14 and 15) in this section are two examples of *norito*, the sacred prayers recited at Shinto shrines to the *kami* by priests, and which seek the grace of the *kami* while expressing some of the inner meanings of Shinto.

Rituals are extremely important in Japan, and nowhere more so than in Shinto. *Norito*, which are a central element in such rituals, are composed by Shinto priests often in a style based on early Japanese writing styles. Their origins are rooted in early Shinto history, with many of them dating from the time of the *Kojiki*.

The first example given here is an early *norito* and shows the concern with purification and exorcism that is a constant issue in Shinto. The second one is a more modern type composed prior to the war (as were a large number of the *norito* currently in use in Japan) and widely used at shrines throughout Japan. This prayer seeks the help of the *kami* in growing a good harvest, and manifests the emphasis that is placed in Shinto on seeking the support of the *kami* in all fields of human endeavour and in ensuring continued fertility and production.

Reading No. 9
Extracts from the *Kojiki*

SELECTIONS FROM THE TRANSLATION OF THE *KOJIKI* BY DONALD PHILIPPI, WITH APPENDED COMMENTARY ON THE TEXT BY IAN READER

The *Kojiki*, composed in A.D. 712 at the behest of the Imperial Court, outlines a series of mythic legends concerning the *kami*, and the creation of Japan and the Japanese people. The text was written on behalf of the Imperial Court and one of its aims was to justify and legitimate the rule of the Court and Emperor. To do so it forged a direct link between the Emperor and the *kami* by depicting a mythological process of creation in which the Imperial household descended from the Sun Goddess Amaterasu; this mythical descent is at the core of the nationalistic elements of Shinto mentioned earlier.

The *Kojiki* is not just a text justifying Imperial rule, however, for woven into the myths and legends it relates are a number of concepts that express some of the central themes of Shinto and of all Japanese religiosity. There is, for instance, no single Creator figure (unlike, for example, in Christianity): in this first extract (A) we encounter a group of deities who come into existence and then produce two further deities, a male and female, whom they order (B) to create and give order to the land (of Japan).

[A] THE FIVE SEPARATE HEAVENLY DEITIES COME INTO EXISTENCE

At the time of the beginning of heaven and earth, there came into existence in TAKAMA-NÖ-PARA a deity named AMË-NÖ-MI-NAKA-NUSI-NÖ-KAMÏ; next, TAKA-MÏ-MUSUBI-NÖ-KAMÏ; next, KAMÏ-MUSUBI-NÖ-KAMÏ. These three deities all came into existence as single deities, and their forms were not visible.

Next, when the land was young, resembling floating oil and drift-like jellyfish, there sprouted forth something like reed-shoots. From these came into existence the deity UMASI-ASI-KABÏ-PIKO-DI-NÖ-KAMÏ; next AMË-NÖ-TÖKÖ-TATI-NÖ-KAMÏ. These two deities also came into existence as single deities, and their forms were not visible.

The five deities in the above section are the Separate Heavenly Deities.

Izanagi and Izanami create Ongoro Island

[B] IZANAGI AND IZANAMI ARE COMMANDED TO SOLIDIFY THE LAND. THEY CREATE ONŌGÖRÖ ISLAND

At this time the heavenly deities, all with one command, said to the two deities IZANAGI-NÖ-MIKÖTÖ and IZANAMI-NÖ-MIKÖTÖ :

'Complete and solidify this drifting land!'

Giving them the Heavenly Jewelled Spear, they entrusted the mission to them.

Thereupon, the two deities stood on the Heavenly Floating Bridge and, lowering the jewelled spear, stirred with it. They stirred the brine with a churning-churning sound; and when they lifted up [the spear] again, the brine dripping down from the tip of the spear piled up and became an island. This was the island ONŌGŌRŌ.

These two deities then come together to produce various *kami* which populate and give life to the land. This story of procreation giving life to the land and the *kami* puts a very earthy, human side to the process of creation. It is a creation not by one god but by the cooperation and relationship of two, who themselves had been the product of earlier deities. The female deity Izanami, however, dies in childbirth giving birth to the god of fire, and this incident serves to show that *kami* themselves are not necessarily infinite but are subject to some of the trials and tribulations of ordinary mortals. This point is reinforced by the grief of Izanagi, who does not want to lose his partner and so follows her to the world of the dead.

In this next section (C) Izanagi enters the world of the dead, sees his formerly beloved wife Izanami as a rotting corpse, and is then pursued by her (D) as she tries to take him with her. This section brings out the taboos involving death and emphasises the fearful position that it held in early Shinto. It also relays the message that death is a final separation, a fact that is made clear when Izanagi blocks off the world of the dead with a rock, thus drawing a line between the living and the dead.

At the same time the pre-eminence of life over death, and hence the life-affirming nature of Shinto, is stressed when Izanagi, responding to Izanami's threat to kill 1000 people every day, says he will help create 1500 people a day to replace them. The importance of purification as a religious ritual and as a means of regeneration is next brought out (E) with Izanagi bathing after his escape, to cleanse himself from the impurities of the world of the dead. In doing so he gives birth to a number of *kami* including Amaterasu, the Sun Goddess.

[C] IZANAGI VISITS IZANAMI IN THE LAND OF YŌMĪ. BREAKING THE TABOO, HE LOOKS UPON HER CORPSE

At this time, [Izanagi-nö-mikötö], wishing to meet again his spouse IZANAMI-NÖ-MIKÖTÖ, went after her to the land of YŌMĪ.

When she came forth out of the door of the hall to greet him, IZANAGI-NÖ-MIKÖTO said:

'O, my beloved spouse, the lands which you and I were making have not yet been completed; you must come back!'

Then IZANAMI-NÖ-MIKÖTÖ replied, saying:

'How I regret that you did not come sooner. I have eaten at the hearth of YŌMĪ. But, O my beloved husband, how awesome it is that you have entered here! Therefore I will go and discuss for a

71

while with the gods of YŌMĪ my desire to return. Pray do not look upon me!'

Thus saying, she went back into the hall, but her absence was so long that [Izanagi-nö-mikötö] could no longer wait.

Thereupon he broke off one of the large end-teeth of the comb he was wearing in his left hair-bunch, lit [it as] one fire, and entered in to see.

At this time, maggots were squirming and roaring [in the corpse of Izanami-nö-mikötö].

In her head was Great-Thunder;
In her breast was Fire-Thunder;
In her belly was Black-Thunder;
In her genitals was Crack-Thunder;
In her left hand was Young-Thunder;
In her right hand was Earth-Thunder;
In her left foot was Sounding-Thunder;
In her right foot was Reclining-Thunder.
Altogether there were eight thunder-deities.

Finally, his spouse IZANAMI-NÖ-MIKÖTÖ herself came in pursuit of him. Then he pulled a tremendous boulder and closed [the pass] YÖMÖ-TU-PIRA-SAKA with it.

They stood facing each other, one on each side of the boulder, and broke their troth.

At this time IZANAMI-NÖ-MIKÖTÖ said:

'O my beloved husband, if you do thus, I will each day strangle to death one thousand of the populace of your country.'

To this IZANAGI-NÖ-MIKÖTÖ said:

'O my beloved spouse, if you do thus, I will each day build one thousand five hundred parturition huts.'

This is the reason why one thousand people inevitably die and one thousand five hundred people are inevitably born every day.

[E] IZANAGI PURIFIES HIMSELF, GIVING BIRTH TO MANY DEITIES INCLUDING AMA-TERASU-OPO-MI-KAMI AND SUSA-NÖ-WO

Hereupon, IZANAGI-NÖ-OPO-KAMĪ said:

'I have been to a most unpleasant land, a horrible, unclean land. Therefore I shall purify myself.'

Arriving at [the plain] APAKI-PARA by the river-mouth of TATI-BANA in PIMUKA in TUKUSI, he purified and exorcised himself.

In purifying himself with water a number of deities are produced. The last sequence of births is described as follows:

Then when he washed his left eye, there came into existence a deity named AMA-TERASU-OPO-MI-KAMĪ.

Next, when he washed his right eye, there came into existence a deity named TUKU-YŌMI-NŌ-MIKŌTŌ.

Next, when he washed his nose, there came into existence a deity named TAKE-PAYA-SUSA-NŌ-WO-NŌ-MIKŌTŌ.

The fourteen deities in the above section from YA-SO-MAGA-TU-PI-NŌ-KAMĪ through PAYA-SUSA-NŌ-WO-NŌ-MIKŌTŌ, are deities born from bathing his body.

Izanagi entrusts these deities to rule over different realms (F) but Susa-no-wo, the brother of Amaterasu, angry because she has been given a more important role than him, refuses to do what he has been told (G). Izanagi banishes him: after doing this Izanagi plays little further part in the myths.

[F] IZANAGI ENTRUSTS THEIR MISSIONS TO THE THREE NOBLE CHILDREN

At this time IZANAGI-NŌ-MIKŌTŌ, rejoicing greatly, said: 'I have borne child after child, and finally in the last bearing I have obtained three noble children.'

Then he removed his necklace, shaking the beads on the string so that they jingled, and, giving it to AMA-TERASU-OPO-MI-KAMĪ, he entrusted her with her mission, saying:

'You shall rule TAKAMA-NŌ-PARA.'

The name of this necklace is MI-KURA-TANA-NŌ-KAMĪ.

Next he said to TUKU-YŌMI-NŌ-MIKŌTŌ, entrusting him with his mission:

'You shall rule the realms of the night.'

Next he said to TAKE-PAYA-SUSA-NŌ-WO-NŌ-MIKŌTŌ, entrusting him with his mission:

'You shall rule the ocean.'

[G] SUSA-NŌ-WO DISOBEYS HIS DIVINE TRUST AND IS EXPELLED BY IZANAGI

While [the other deities] ruled [their realms] in obedience to the commands entrusted to them, PAYA-SUSA-NŌ-WO-NŌ-MIKŌTŌ did not rule the land entrusted to him. [Instead], he wept and howled [even] until his beard eight hands long extended down over his chest.

His weeping was such that it caused the verdant mountains to

Torii at Itsukushima Shrine, Miyajima

wither and all the rivers and seas to dry up. At this, the cries of malevolent deities were everywhere abundant like summer flies; and all sorts of calamities arose in all things.

Then IZANAGI-NŌ-OPO-MI-KAMĪ said to PAYA-SUSA-NŌ-WO-NŌ-MIKŌTŌ:

'Why is it you do not rule the land entrusted to you, but [instead] weep and howl?'

Then [PAYA-SUSA-NŌ-WO-NŌ-MIKŌTŌ] replied:

'I wish to go to the land of my mother, NE-NŌ-KATA-SU-KUNI. That is why I weep.'

Then IZANAGI-NŌ-OPO-MI-KAMĪ, greatly enraged, said:

'In that case, you may not live in this land!'

Thus [saying], he expelled him with a divine expulsion.

However, Susa-no-wo refuses to accept banishment, returning to cause further trouble and challenge his sister's authority. He breaks every rule of behaviour, culminating in the act of flaying a horse (a holy animal) and flinging it into her room (H). This is the ultimate insult and a breach of ritual purity designed to insult Amaterasu.

The behaviour of Susa-no-wo shows both the potentially dangerous qualities of the *kami*, who if not treated with respect can cause problems, and their human nature: Susa-no-wo's anger is somewhat reminiscent of a child who has not been given what he wants.

[H] SUSA-NÖ-WO RAGES WITH VICTORY

Then PAYA-SUSA-NÖ-WO-NÖ-MIKÖTÖ said to AMA-TERASU-OPO-MI-KAMĪ:

'It was because my intentions were pure and bright that in the children I begot I obtained graceful maidens. By this it is obvious that I have won.'

Thus saying, he raged with victory, breaking down the ridges between the rice paddies of AMA-TERASU-OPO-MI-KAMĪ and covering up the ditches.

Also he defecated and strewed the faeces about in the hall where the first fruits were tasted.

Even though he did this, AMA-TERASU-OPO-MI-KAMĪ did not reprove him, but said:

'That which appears to be faeces must be what my brother has vomited and strewn about while drunk. Also his breaking down the ridges of the paddies and covering up their ditches - my brother must have done this because he thought it was wasteful to use the land thus.'

Even though she thus spoke with good intention, his misdeeds did not cease, but became even more flagrant.

When AMA-TERASU-OPO-MI-KAMĪ was inside the sacred weaving hall seeing to the weaving of the divine garments, he opened a hole in the roof of the sacred weaving hall and dropped down into it the heavenly dappled pony which he had skinned with a backwards skinning.

The heavenly weaving maiden, seeing this, was alarmed and struck her genitals against the shuttle and died.

Amaterasu's response to the insult shows similar childishness: she withdraws from the world and sulks in a cave. Because she is the Sun Goddess her absence throws the world into darkness (I).

[I] AMA-TERASU-OPO-MI-KAMĪ CONCEALS HERSELF. THE OTHER DEITIES LURE HER OUT. SUSA-NÖ-WO IS EXPELLED

At this time, AMA-TERASU-OPO-MI-KAMĪ, seeing this, was afraid, and opening the heavenly rock-cave door, went in and shut herself inside.

Then TAKAMA-NÖ-PARA was completely dark, and the Central Land of the Reed Plains was entirely dark.

Because of this, constant night reigned, and the cries of the myriad deities were everywhere abundant, like summer flies; and all manner of calamities arose.

The other *kami* try all sorts of ways of getting her out, until eventually she emerges out of curiosity as she hears the other *kami* laughing when one of the female *kami* performs a lewd dance. This mythical event is commemorated by sacred dances performed by shrine maidens (although now with no lewd content) that are a part of most Shinto rituals, and that are used to symbolically invoke the presence of the *kami*.

Then AMA-TERASU-OPO-MI-KAMĪ, thinking this more and more strange, gradually came out of the door and approached [the mirror.]

Then the hidden AMË-NÖ-TA-DIKARA-WO-NÖ-KAMĪ took her hand and pulled her out. Immediately PUTO-TAMA-NÖ-MIKÖTÖ extended a SIRI-KUMË rope behind her, and said:

'You may go back no further than this!'

When AMA-TERASU-OPO-MI-KAMĪ came forth, TAKAMA-NÖ-PARA and the Central Land of the Reed Plains of themselves became light.

At this time the eight-hundred myriad deities deliberated together, imposed upon PAYA-SUSA-NÖ-WO-NÖ-MIKÖTÖ a fine of a thousand tables of restitutive gifts, and also, cutting off his beard and the nails of his hands and feet, had him exorcised and expelled him with a divine expulsion.

After this sequence of episodes the myths relate how the world became tranquil and peaceful, after which Ninigi the grandson of Amaterasu is commanded to descend to earth as its ruler. He is entrusted with the imperial regalia including the sacred mirror that is the symbol of Amaterasu. According to Shinto belief this sacred mirror is enshrined at Ise. Ninigi's great-grandson, according to the myths, is Jimmu, the first Emperor of Japan, who is entrusted with guarding the imperial regalia and the sacred mirror.

According to the legends, and in the eyes of Japanese nationalists, all subsequent Emperors have descended from Jimmu. As such the myths related in the *Kojiki* show the Japanese Emperor to be a direct descendant of Amaterasu, a 'fact' that later was extremely important in the promotion of the veneration of the Emperor during the period of State Shinto in the earlier part of this century (see, for example, Reading No. 47 in Chapter Eight).

Reading No. 10
The meaning of kami

By DANIEL HOLTOM

No other word in the entire range of Japanese vocabularly has a richer or more varied content and no other has presented greater difficulties to the philologist than the word kami.

The most comprehensive and penetrating account of the meaning of kami that has appeared in Japanese literature was given by the great eighteenth-century scholar, Motoori Norinaga. Written long before the age of the modern study of folk psychology had dawned, his analysis, in spite of certain insufficiencies, yet may be taken to stand as a remarkable and almost classical definition of the now widely used term mana.

He says:

'I do not yet understand the meaning of the term, kami. Speaking in general, however, it may be said that kami signifies, in the first place, the deities of heaven and earth that appear in the ancient records and also the spirits of the shrines where they are worshipped.

'It is hardly necessary to say that it includes human beings. It also includes such objects as birds, beasts, trees, plants, seas, mountains and so forth. In ancient usage, anything whatsoever which was outside the ordinary, which possessed superior power or which was awe-inspiring was called kami. Eminence here does not refer merely to the superiority of nobility, goodness or meritorious deeds. Evil and mysterious things, if they are extraordinary and dreadful, are called kami. It is needless to say that among human beings who are called kami the successive generations of sacred emperors are all included.

'The fact that emperors are also called "distant kami" is because, from the standpoint of common people, they are far-separated, majestic and worthy of reverence. In a lesser degree we find, in the present as well as in ancient times, human beings who are kami. Although they may not be accepted throughout the whole country, yet in each province, each village and each family there are human beings who are kami, each one according to his own proper position. The kami of the divine age were for the most part human beings of that time and, because the people of that time were all kami, it

Tree *kami* (holy tree) in Kyoto

is called the Age of the Gods (*kami*).

'Furthermore, among things which are not human, the thunder is always called "sounding *kami*". Such things as dragons, the echo, and foxes, inasmuch as they are conspicuous, wonderful and awe-inspiring, are also *kami*. In popular usage the echo is said to be *tengu* [a magical, long-nosed goblin said to live in the mountains] and in Chinese writings it is referred to as a mountain goblin....

'In the *Nihongi* and the *Manyōshū* the tiger and the wolf are also spoken of as *kami*. Again there are the cases in which peaches were given the name, August-Thing-Great-*Kamu*-Fruit, and a necklace was called August-Storehouse-Shelf-*Kami*. There are further instances in which rocks, stumps of trees and leaves of plants spoke audibly. They were all *kami*. There are again numerous places in which seas and mountains are called *kami*. This does not have reference to the spirit of the mountain or the sea, but *kami* is used here directly of the particular mountain or sea. This is because they were exceedingly awe-inspiring.'

Much similar material could be adduced from Japanese sources. It is impossible to consider it within the scope of the present discussion. Summarised briefly, it may be said that *kami* is essentially an expression used by the early Japanese people to classify experiences that evoked sentiments of caution and mystery in the

78

presence of the manifestation of the strange and marvellous. Like numerous other concepts discoverable among ancient or primitive peoples, *kami* is fundamentally a term that distinguishes between a world of superior beings and things which are thought of as filled with mysterious power and a world of common experiences that lie within the control of ordinary human technique. Often the best translation is simply by the word 'sacred'. In this sense it has an undifferentiated background of everything that is strange, fearful, mysterious, marvellous, uncontrolled, full of power, or beyond human comprehension.

The conviction of the reality of the world that it registered was supported by the experience of extraordinary events, such as the frenzy of religious dances, or by outstanding objects that threw the attention into special activity, such as large, or old, or strangely formed trees, high mountains, thunder, lightning, storm and clouds, or by implements of magic, or by uncanny animals, such as foxes, badgers, and manifestations of albinism. These old attitudes exist in the present and strongly influence modern Shinto.

As this sacred, mysterious background became more and more articulated with the progress of experience and thought, descriptive elements were attached to the word, *kami*, and the names of the great deities were evolved, as, for example, *Amaterasu-Ōmikami*, 'Heaven-shining-Great-August-*Kami*', for the Sun Goddess, or *Taka-Mimusubi-no-Kami*, 'High-August-Producing-*Kami*', the name given one of the creation deities or growth principles of the old cosmogonic myth.

In addition to the general sense of sacred as just outlined, the specific meanings of *kami* should be noted. They are: spirits and deities of nature; the spirits of ancestors (especially great ancestors, including emperors, heroes, wise men and saints); superior human beings in actual human society, such as living emperors, high government officials, feudal lords, etc.; the government itself; that which is above in space or superior in location or rank (declared, without warrant, by some Japanese scholars to be the primary meaning); 'the upper times', i.e., antiquity; God; the hair on the human scalp; paper.

Evidence which cannot be cited here goes to show that the classification of the hair on the human scalp under the *kami* concept had probable origin, not in the very apparent fact that the hair was on the top of the head and hence 'superior', but in the association of the hair with a primitive supernaturalism or with the idea of mysterious superhuman force.

Reading No. 11

Ise - the sun shrine

By SVEND HVASS

Grand shrine at Ise. Photo: Kyodo News Service

In 685 Emperor Temmu ordered that his most important Shinto shrine, Ise, was to be rebuilt every 20th year as an exact copy of the old shrine so that the buildings always would be the most distinguished in the country. Possibly in the first centuries of its existence the shrine was now and then moved (in early Japanese history it was customary to move the capital at the death of an emperor) in order to renew the wood, the life span of which, in a building with pillars sunk into the ground itself, is of limited endurance.

Subsequently, the reconstructions were systematised and with few interruptions they have continued since then. The inauguration of the 60th complex of buildings, for example, started on 2 October 1973. Although brand new, the structures, with very few alterations, represent a way of building which is more than a thousand years old - a type of architecture which came into being before the influence from the Asian continent manifested itself and which ever since has maintained its form. In architecture and in cultural history this must be considered as unique.

One would expect that such buildings would be enormous and gaudy in order to emphasise the power of the emperor and the importance of his family relationship to the sun. But in reality they are modest buildings, in size, materials and form. The main buildings cover an area of less than 15 by 9 metres, and from the ground to the top of the rafters, the *chigi* is about 12 metres. The pillars, which are sunk right into the earth, and the other woodwork are made of *hinoki*, Japanese cypress; they are left undressed and unpainted and have only a few decorations which are later additions.

In no way, however, do they take away from the great and honest simplicity of the buildings in which the amazing skill of the carpenters and their precision in shaping the wood stand out as its most important kind of decoration.

The buildings have simple, thatched roofs, carefully cut and almost one metre deep. Across the ridge of the roof there rest nine (in the Outer Shrine) or 10 (in the Inner) rolls of wood called *katsuogi* (an architectural form that remains from the time when it was necessary to put 'weights' on the roof to keep it down when there were storms and typhoons). These *katsuogi* are now only used in Shinto shrines, where the number of them indicate the importance of the building they are placed on, and in a few Imperial buildings. This style is called *yuiitsu-shinmei-zukuri*, or 'The Only Divine Style' and is a type of architecture which, after the building of Ise (seventh century), was ever after prohibited from being used or copied in other buildings.

The approach to the buildings is interesting, especially to the inner shrine, Naiku, which is situated four miles from Geku, the outer shrine, on the other side of the Isuzu River. The holy grounds are large and one must walk over half a mile at the Naiku shrine before one gets to the buildings themselves. One crosses the very beautiful Uji Bridge which is also renewed every 20th year, and first walks on broad, laid-out paths.

As is generally the case in Japanese gardens, the walking surfaces are a matter of deliberate choice. Here it consists of pebbles that

Of the affiliated shrines at Ize on the Izuzu River is the one dedicated to Amaterasu-Omikami at Naiku (inner shrine)

crunch under the feet so that conversation becomes difficult which in turn leads your thoughts inward, towards the divine. A bit further on the path passes the river and at this spot, Mitarashi, you put your hands in the water, and then, having walked a little bit further on, you take a sip of water from the delicately carved dipper as is customary at all Shinto shrines so that you can be purified ritually. Here the river is as much part of the shrine as the buildings themselves.

You now walk away from the broad paths and enter a grove. Surrounded by enormous cypresses and cedars you become aware of a different feeling or mood. I remember that when I first came here, I heard some deep, thudding, drum-like sounds at different pitches in the distance. I was sure that some religious dances or the like had begun and I stood listening to this faraway sound for a long time - a sound which fitted the scenery and the mood of the place so well. When I got nearer, however, I found that the sound came from some Ise carpenters working on a bridge. Every time they applied their tools on a piece of wood they fell into step and continued so until suddenly all stopped as if under command, quite probably maintaining a sound and a rhythm, that has been heard from time to time in exactly the same way for about 1500 years. The carpenters of Ise always wear immaculate white clothes (the colour of purity). They often bathe to become physically and spiritually purified, and should blood, for any reason, fall on a piece of wood it is discarded as unfit as it is no longer pure.

Then you reach the shrine itself, well hidden behind four high fences (so-called 'curtains') in an area of slightly more than 105 by 45 metres. Next to it there is a similar piece of ground of the same size, and it is here that a new group of buildings is being built so that every 20th years the shrine is moved from one place to the other. For the last six years dozens of carpenters have worked on the new buildings, the holy of holies and two storerooms. Four gates lead to them. Three of them on line, whereas the last is moved away from the symmetrical axis. To make it all symmetrical would be too perfect and would amount to boasting. The totally perfect belongs to the gods alone so that it is traditional for the carpenters to add some minor 'mistake' such as this.

Very few ordinary men are allowed to enter these gates. Information about the buildings, therefore, is invariably second-hand. (Only a tiny part of the roof ridges can be seen from the outside.)

Ordinary people are not allowed in the holy grounds and this is something all Japanese have long felt should be respected. That this is so was emphasised when the then Minister of Education, Mori, on 11 February 1889, the same day Japan got its first free constitution, was killed by a Shinto fanatic who had heard that Mori had prodded some curtains with his stick in order to get a glimpse of the holy religious ceremonies enacted behind them.

The murderer, Nishino, who was immediately beheaded by one of the minister's men, was buried in the Yanaka graveyard, but shortly after the authorities had to forbid admittance to his grave. People went on pilgrimage to the place as if it was an important shrine and all sympathy was on the murderer Nishino's side, and certainly not on the minister's who was thought to have broken one of the state's unwritten religious laws.

Only high-ranking priests and priestesses, members of the Imperial family and its special emissaries, are allowed here. In the holy of holies only the Emperor and the High Priestess are allowed entrance. Until at least the fourteenth century, these high priestesses were always virgin daughters of an emperor and they had to lead a chaste and decent life in the service of the Sun Goddess.

It has always been customary for the Emperor or his representative to visit Ise on the occasion of important national events so that he can inform the Sun Goddess about such matters personally. Also government ministers (even in modern times) have paid a visit here on taking office to get their appointment confirmed. The previous Emperor, Hirohito, kept the Sun Goddess informed more than many of his predecessors. The first time he was at Ise was immediately before his first voyage to Europe in 1921 as the Crown Prince. He returned when he got married, when he was crowned, and on several occasions when Japan had won major battles before and during the Second World War. In the middle of November 1945 he came with a heavy heart to Ise's inner shrine because on this occasion he had to explain to Amaterasu the reasons for Japan's defeat in the Pacific War and also offer his apologies.

The most sacred symbol at Ise is a holy mirror, one of the symbols of the gods. The mirror, or rather the remnants of it, is the 'secret of secrets', and is always enveloped in silk, and never seen. It symbolises the presence of the Sun Goddess, and at the great Sengushiki ceremony when the new shrine has been rebuilt (the next occasion is in 1993) it will be transported to the new building, not directly but via another building where food and other things are being sacrificed. This careful transference helps the Goddess adjust to the new shrine, and helps guarantee the sense of renewal, purity and continuity which the shrines of Ise symbolise.

Reading No 12
A pilgrimage to Ise

By THE BUDDHIST MONK, SAKA 14th Century

When on the way to these shrines you do not feel like an ordinary person any longer but as though reborn in another world. How solemn is the unearthly shadow of the huge groves of ancient pines and chamaecyparis, and there is also a delicate pathos in the few rare flowers that have withstood the winter frosts so well.

The cross-beam of the *torii* or Shinto gateway is without any curve, symbolising by its straightness the sincerity of the direct beam of the Divine promise. The shrine-fence is not painted red nor is the shrine itself roofed with cedar shingles. The eaves, with their rough reed-thatch, recall memories of the ancient days when the roofs were not trimmed. So did they spare expense out of compassion for the hardships of the people.

Within the shrine there are many buildings where the festival rites are performed, constructed just like those in the Imperial Palace. Buddhist monks may go only as far as the Sacred Tree known as the Cryptomeria of the Five Hundred Branches (*loe-no-sugi*). They may not go to the shrine. This, too, is a ceremonial rule of the Imperial Court....

When I went to worship at the Shrine of the Moon-Deity Tsukiyomi the fallen leaves in the grove covered my traces and the winter powdered the foliage in the court. And the name of Tsukiyomi recalled so vividly the age of the deities that I was inspired to write:

> *How many long years*
> *Has this ancient shrine-fence stood*
> *Wet with countless dews,*
> *And the Moon of the Gods' age*
> *Is this selfsame autumn moon.*

I fear that my clumsy pen can hardly do justice to the road from Yamada to the inner Shrine. Sometimes the spray over the hills seems to reflect their reversed silhouettes, sometimes the way is shrouded in cloud so that the countless peaks of the hills are hidden.

As we approach the village of Uji the name is welcome to us with its suggestion of nearness to the Capital, and as it lies under the hills at the south-west of the Outer Shrine it is a place where you might imagine people would make cottages to live in retirement. As we went on deep in the shade of the chamaecyparis groves there was not even the smoke of any habitation to be seen, and we felt as though we had suddenly transcended the bounds of this painful world, while the hills with their cloud-capped mystery transported us to the world of Taoist fairyland.

When I entered the second *torii* or Shinto gateway to worship it was dark under the pines at the foot of the hill and the branches were so thick-matted that one could hardly discern the Pine of One Hundred Branches. The cryptomerias within the shrine precincts were so dense that even the oblique projecting roof-beams could hardly be made out. When I came to reflect on my condition my mind is full of the Ten Evils and I felt shame at so long forsaking the will of Buddha, yet as I wear one of the three monkish robes, I must feel some chagrin at my estrangement from the Way of the Deities.

In particular is it the long-established custom of this shrine not to bring in any Buddhist rosary or offering, or any special petition in our hearts; this is called 'Inner Purity'. Washing in sea water and keeping the body free from all defilement is called 'Outer Purity'. And when both these Purities are attained there is then no barrier between our mind and that of the Deity. And if we feel to become thus one with the Divine, what more do we need and what is there to pray for? When I heard that this was the true way of worshipping at the shrine, I could not refrain from shedding tears of gratitude.

□□□□

Reading No. 13

Meiji Jingu and the traditional plan of a Shinto shrine

By FINN STEFÁNSSON

Meiji Jingu (*jingu* = shrine) is situated in the midst of a large wooded area in central Tokyo. It was built in 1920 to commemorate Emperor Meiji (1868-1912) and Empress Shoken (d. 1914). The grounds have more than 100,000 trees and bushes, given as gifts from different parts of Japan, so that all types of trees are represented. The buildings themselves are made of cypress wood from Kiso, considered to be the best timber in Japan.

The photo (page 86) shows the central parts of the shrine, 'the inner garden', but there is also an 'outer garden' with a building where Shinto weddings are held, and a number of sports grounds (used at the Olympic Games in 1964).

In the innermost building called *honden*[6] the Emperor and the Empress are enshrined as *kami*, and it is these *kami* the visitors honour and worship - daily, at family feasts or at New Year.

A brochure from the shrine gives the following rules for praying at the shrine:

'a. Be suitably clothed for the occasion. Walk through the *torii* (the gateway)[1] and along the *sando* (the path to the shrine)[2].

b. Go to the *temizuya* (a stone purification basin)[3] and wash your hands thoroughly. Pour water from the wooden dipper into the hollow of your hand and take the water into your mouth and gargle. (Do not take the wooden dipper up to your lips).

c. Go to the counter at the *haiden* (the outer hall with a platform on which ceremonies are performed)[5] having passed Minami Shinmon (Great Southern Gate)[4]. Stand facing the enshrined *kami*. Drop some money (notes or coins) into the sacrificial chest.

d. Bow low twice.

e. Clap your hands twice.

f. Bow low once more.'

In the side wings between the outer hall and the southern gate there is, among other things, a booth for selling oracles, the small pieces of paper that tell one's fortune and that are hung on the holy *sakaki* trees near by after they have been read.

Taken from a leaflet given out at the shrine.

□□□□

Reading No. 14
Norito: a Shinto prayer of exorcism
GREAT EXORCISM OF THE LAST DAY OF THE SIXTH MONTH
(Minaduki tugomori no oho-harahe)

Hear me, all of you assembled princes of the blood, princes, court nobles, and all officials. Thus I speak.

The various sins perpetrated and committed
    By those who serve in the Emperor's court,
        The scarf-wearing women attendants,
        The sash-wearing men attendants,
        The quiver-bearing guard attendants,
        The sword-bearing guard attendants,
    As well as all those who serve in various offices -
These sins are to be exorcised, are to be purified
    In the great exorcism of the last day of the sixth month
        of this year -
Hear me, all of you. Thus I speak.

By the command of the Sovereign Ancestral Gods and Goddesses,
    Who divinely remain in the High Heavenly Plain,
The eight myriad deities were convoked in a divine convocation,
    Consulted in a divine consultation,
    And spoke these words of entrusting:
        'Our Sovereign Grandchild is to rule
        'The Land of the Plentiful Reed Plains of the Fresh Ears
        of Grain
        'Tranquilly as a peaceful land.'
Having thus entrusted the land,
    They inquired with a divine inquiry
    Of the unruly deities in the land,
    And expelled them with a divine expulsion;
They silenced to the last leaf
    The rocks and the stumps of the trees,
    Which had been able to speak,
And caused him to descend from the heavens,

Leaving the heavenly rock-seat,
And pushing with an awesome pushing
   Through the myriad layers of heavenly clouds -
Thus they entrusted [the land to him].

The lands of the four quarters thus entrusted,
   Great Yamato, the Land of the Sun-Seen-on-High,
   Was pacified and made a peaceful land;
The palace posts were firmly planted in the bed-rock below,
   The cross-beams soaring high towards the High Heavenly Plain,
   And the noble palace of the Sovereign Grandchild constructed,
     Where, as a heavenly shelter, as a sun-shelter,
      he dwells hidden.
     And rules [the kingdom] tranquilly as a peaceful land.

The various sins perpetrated and committed
   By the heavenly ever-increasing people to come into existence
   In this land which he is to rule tranquilly as a peaceful land:
First, the heavenly sins:
   Breaking down the ridges,
   Covering up the ditches,
   Releasing the irrigation sluices,
   Double planting,
   Setting up stakes,
   Skinning alive, skinning backwards,
   Defecation -
   Many sins [such as these] are distinguished and called the
     heavenly sins:
The earthly sins:
   Cutting living flesh, cutting dead flesh,
   White leprosy, skin excrescences,
   The sin of violating one's own mother,
   The sin of violating one's own child,
   The sin of violating a mother and her child,
   The sin of violating a child and her mother,
   The sin of transgression with animals,
   Woes from creeping insects,
   Woes from the deities of on high,
   Woes from the birds of on high,
   Killing animals, the sin of witchcraft -
   Many sins [such as these] shall appear.

When they thus appear,
By the heavenly shrine usage,
   Let the Great Nakatomi cut off the bottom and cut off the top

Of heavenly narrow pieces of wood,
And place them in abundance on a thousand tables;
Let him cut off the bottom and cut off the top
    Of heavenly sedge reeds
And cut them up into myriad strips;
And let him pronounce the heavenly ritual, the solemn
    ritual words.
When he thus pronounces them,
    The heavenly deities will push open the heavenly rock door,
    And pushing with an awesome pushing
        Through the myriad layers of heavenly clouds,
    Will hear and receive [these words].
Then the earthly deities will climb up
    To the summits of the high mountains and to the summits of
    the low mountains,
    And pushing aside the mists of the high mountains and the
    mists of the low mountains,
    Will hear and receive [these words].

When they thus hear and receive,
Then, beginning with the court of the Sovereign Grandchild,
    In the lands of the four quarters under the heavens,
    Each and every sin will be gone.
As the gusty wind blows apart the myriad layers of heavenly clouds;
    As the morning mist, the evening mist is blown away by the
        morning wind, the evening wind;
    As the large ship anchored in the spacious port is untied
        at the prow and untied at the stern
            And pushed out into the great ocean;
    As the luxuriant clump of trees on yonder [hill]
        Is cut away at the base with a tempered sickle, a sharp sickle -
As a result of the exorcism and the purification,
    There will be no sins left.
They will be taken into the great ocean
    By the goddess called Se-ori-tu-hime,
    Who dwells in the rapids of the rapid-running rivers
        Which fall surging perpendicular
        From the summits of the high mountains and the summits
            of the low mountains.
When she thus takes them,
    They will be swallowed with a gulp
        By the goddess called Haya-aki-tu-hime,
            Who dwells in the wild brine, the myriad currents
            of the brine.
                In the myriad meeting-places of the brine of

the many briny currents.
When she thus swallows them with a gulp,
    The deity called Ibuki-do-nusi,
        Who dwells in the Ibuki-do, [lit. 'breath-blowing' entrance]
    Will blow them away with his breath to the land of Hades,
    the under-world.
When he thus blows them away,
    The deity called Haya-sasura-hime,
        Who dwells in the land of Hades, the under-world,
    Will wander off with them and lose them.
When she thus loses them,
    Beginning with the many officials serving in the Emperor's
    court,
    In the four quarters under the heavens,
    Beginning from today,
    Each and every sin will be gone.
Holding the horses
    Which stand listening,
      Pricking up their ears towards the High Heavenly Plain,
Hear me, all of you:
Know that [all the sins] have been exorcised and purified
    In the great exorcism performed in the waning of the evening
    sun
    On the last day of the sixth month of this year. Thus I speak.

Oh diviners of the four lands,
    Carry them out to the great river
    And cast them away. Thus I speak.

Reading No. 15
Norito: a prayer for good crops

Traditional food offerings

'In the dread presence, before the sacred shrine (name of shrine is here inserted), the chief of the shrine (name and rank of priest are here inserted), with trembling makes utterance: Now that His Imperial Majesty, about to make beginning of the (rice) crop for this year, has caused offerings to be presented in abundance, do we (coming) cleansed and purified into thy great presence, make offerings - of food offerings: soft rice and rough rice [i.e., hulled rice and unhulled rice]; of drink offerings: making high the tops of the wine jars and arranging in full rows the bellies of the wine jars; of things that live in the blue sea-plain: things broad of fin and things narrow of fin, even to grasses of the offing and grasses of the shore - all these do we offer in abundance; and, as the full and glorious sun of this day of life and plenty rises, do thou hear to the end these words of praise, in tranquillity and peace. (Grant that) all things that may be grown, beginning with the late-ripening rice which will be produced by the people (lit., great treasure of the land) by stirring with arms and hands the foamy waters and by drawing the mud together between the opposing thighs, and extending even to the part blade of grass, (grant that they) may not meet with evil winds or violent waters; prosper them with abundance and luxuriance, and make the Festival of New Food [Niiname Sai] to be celebrated in sublimity and loveliness. Thus, with dread, we declare the ending of the words of praise.'

5

Buddhism

By IAN READER

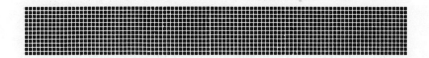

Buddhism originated over 2500 years ago when the historical
Buddha sat in meditation at Buddh Gaya in northern India and
became enlightened. In this state of mind he understood the nature
of existence, realising that the cause of man's suffering was desire,
and that the way to overcome suffering was to vanquish desire. He
therefore preached a path of abstinence and meditation that led
one from suffering to the world of the transcendent realisation
known as enlightenment.

This teaching became known as Buddhism, and he came to be
known as the Buddha (the title means 'the enlightened one'). The
creed he taught took root first in northern India and then spread
to Sri Lanka and South-East Asia. Later, it also went north, across
the Himalayas into Tibet, as well as across the deserts of Central
Asia and into China and Korea. From there it spread, one thousand
years after its initial formation, into Japan.

Along the way, Buddhism developed a complex textual tradition
and many profound philosophical systems, schools of thought,
religious practices and figures of worship. It developed into two
major branches, Theravada (also known as Hinayana) Buddhism,
which flourished in Southern Asia, and Mahayana Buddhism, which
was prominent in the Far East and Tibet. Both forms taught that
all beings would pass through a seemingly endless cycle of births
and rebirths and remain in the world of suffering unless and until
they could overcome desire and achieve enlightenment.

Todaiji Temple, Nara. Photo: John Greenlees

Theravada, though, was more monastically inclined, teaching strict adherence to religious rules and precepts, and considering that enlightenment was out of the reach of all but a very few monks. Mahayana Buddhism, on the other hand, said that all beings contained within them the potential to become enlightened. It taught the paramount importance of compassion and talked of a vast pantheon of compassionate Buddha figures who could help all those who worshipped them.

It was Mahayana Buddhism with its numerous compassionate Buddhas and its vast array of practices, including worship of the Buddhas, that entered and took root in Japan in the sixth century. Since then it has developed at many different levels, having a profound effect in the world of Japanese religions. At popular and folk levels, as was seen in Chapter Three, it has been active as a medium for dealing with the spirits of the dead and with the ancestors, with the *butsudan* (family Buddhist altar) being a common feature in Japanese houses. Its compassionate Buddha figures such as Jizo and Kannon, both also mentioned in Chapter Three, have become popular folk deities to whom people pray in times of need.

Buddhism has also developed its own powerful schools of thought in Japan, and has developed a rich tradition not just of philosophy but also of practice. Buddhism, as with other Japanese religions, is not concerned with philosophy as such, but with the means of putting philosophy into action. As a result, it preaches the importance of the performance of religious practices such as meditation, the recitation of prayers and acts of worship.

AN OUTLINE OF THE READINGS

The readings in this chapter show some of the breadth of Buddhism's philosophical development in Japan along with the religious practices that have evolved from it. The readings take in many of

Built in the 1970s, the world's tallest image of Buddha, stands at a height of 33 metres and is located at Shirayama, Mie Prefecture, Japan

95

the schools of Buddhism that have flourished in Japan, and we will encounter Shingon Buddhism, Pure Land Buddhism, Nichiren Buddhism and Zen Buddhism in turn. The last of these, Zen, has been singled out for deeper discussion as a representative form of Buddhism in Japan. This is not so much because of size (for Zen counts less members than Pure Land or Nichiren Buddhism) but because Zen is the form of Japanese Buddhism that is most widely known in the West.

The first reading (No. 16) comes from the Lotus Sutra, one of the most popular of all Buddhist texts in the Far East which is used by nearly every Buddhist school of thought in Japan. This text describes in poetic form how Mahayana Buddhism, with its promise of salvation and enlightenment for all, came into being.

The importance of texts such as the Lotus Sutra is affirmed throughout the Buddhism of Japan, but at the same time much emphasis has been placed on rituals and meditational practices. This is especially so in the form of Buddhism known as Shingon ('true word') Buddhism. Shingon uses various objects and signs as aids to meditation and as symbols of power in its rituals. It is also concerned with the *esoteric* (i.e. secret) transmission of knowledge from master to disciple through rituals.

The most important focal elements in Shingon Buddhist practice are *mandalas*, sacred pictorial representations of the universe which are used as guides to meditation and enlightenment. In the second reading (No. 17) we encounter the two *mandalas* of the Shingon tradition and learn about their meanings, use and iconography.

The next two readings (Nos. 18 and 19) also deal with the Shingon tradition and with its founder in Japan, the monk Kukai. Like many of the other great founders of Japanese Buddhist schools, Kukai originally went across to China to study, coming back to Japan with the new teachings he had studied, and then establishing them in Japan.

One of the central ideas in his new teaching was that of *sokushinjobutsu* ('becoming a Buddha in this very body/lifetime'), which taught that one could, through the practices of Shingon ritual, become an enlightened Buddha. This was a challenging new view, and the reading shows how Kukai explains his teaching, not just theoretically but practically, to show its validity.

Kukai (also popularly known as Kobo Daishi, a posthumous title of respect) is one of the great personalities of Japanese religious history, revered not just as a Buddhist leader but as a saintly miracle-worker who has become a popular religious figure of worship in Japan. As a result many stories, legends and religious writings have developed about him.

Reading No. 18 on *sokushinjobutsu* is one such legend: the next reading (No. 19), taken from a religious portrait and talisman of him, shows him in his guise as a figure of worship. In this veneration of holy figures such as Kukai we can see the ways in which the Buddhist tradition becomes mingled with the popular folk religious tradition.

Reading No. 20 comes from the Pure Land Buddhist tradition established by Honen in the twelfth century and later developed by Shinran. Honen and Shinran felt that the traditional meditational practices of Buddhism were too difficult for ordinary people, and preached a simple path of faith in the powers of the Buddha of the Pure Land, Amida.

Statue of Kobo Daishi (Kukai) with offerings

Honen and Shinran believed that the age they were living in was a dark and dismal one in which the Buddhist law was decaying, and in which people could no longer hope for enlightenment. Instead, the only hope for them was to be saved by the infinite mercy of Amida, the Buddha of the Pure Land. People who recited the invocation *Namu Amida Butsu* ('praise to the Buddha Amida') would, they preached, be saved by Amida's grace and would be admitted into Amida's Pure Land at death. This reading is an extract from Honen's last testament outlining the essence of Pure Land Buddhist thought.

Reading No. 21 introduces the Buddhist tradition developed in Japan by the fiery prophet Nichiren. Nichiren's Buddhism is native to Japan and has some strongly nationalistic elements to it. Nichiren, like Honen and Shinran, believed that he was living in a decadent era of Buddhist law and that, without a radical revival, all would be lost. Nichiren's was not just an individual path, however. His teaching sought a national revival in which the whole nation of Japan, through faith in and recitation of the Lotus Sutra, which he saw as containing the essence of all truth, would rise up and create a paradisal Buddha land in this world.

At the time when Nichiren lived, in the thirteenth century, Japan was under threat from invasion by the Mongols and Nichiren believed that only through his teachings, which also sought complete union of Buddhism and the state, could Japan be saved. He proclaimed himself the prophet and saviour of Japan, and said that Japan would, in following the path he preached, become the world centre of a revitalised Buddhism. The reading gives two extracts from his writings outlining is thoughts and also his sense of prophecy.

The last readings (Nos. 22 to 27) centre on Zen Buddhism. Zen, which originated in China at a time when Buddhism had become very formalised, was a movement that sought to return to the early simplicity of Buddhism. It taught a direct approach to truth that could not be found in texts so much as in experience and meditation.

Zen developed many apparently simple, parable-like stories known as *koan* that acted as guides to meditation and to self-awakening, thus revealing the inner messages of Zen. Reading No. 22 provides us with a good example of a Zen teaching story. The Ox-herding pictures are, as Aage Marcus explains, a series of pictures that convey Zen's inner messages about the nature of existence and the search for truth in an often humorous and simple, straightforward manner.

Zen teaches that enlightenment is not a special thing but the basic form of existence, to be found and realised directly in the present, and as such it concentrates on everyday, ordinary things. Zen temple life centres on meditation but does not neglect all other, even basic and ordinary, aspects of life.

Reading No. 23 provides an account of Zen temple life by Poul Erik Pilmann which brings out the 'ordinariness' of temple life and how it seeks to teach monks to appreciate and find true quality in all things around them, in such simple things as having a bath, eating plain food and just sitting still in meditation. Reading No. 24 which follows this provides instructions on how to meditate in the Zen way.

Zen is famous also for its contributions to Japanese culture. The concern for an aesthetic simplicity, which permeates all Zen activities, has had a profound effect on Japanese art, literature and even on its martial arts and physical disciplines, and this effect is illustrated by Readings Nos. 25, 26 and 27.

Many Japanese poets were deeply influenced by Zen, including Basho, the most famous exponent of the 17-syllable poetic form

'Nichiren Shonin Preaching' (Thirteenth century. Myohokkeji Temple, Shizuoka Prefecture.)

known as *haiku*. The selection of *haiku* translated from the Japanese by R. H. Blyth (No. 25) demonstrates the often humorous and vibrant nature of *haiku*. The capacity also of Zen to laugh at itself is brought out by the parody of poem (4), the most famous Japanese *haiku* of all.

Reading No. 26 describes the famous Zen rock garden at Ryoanji in Kyoto and shows how Zen is expressed also through such art-forms as landscape gardening, and how gardens themselves can provide Zen teachings on life.

The last reading (No. 27) in this chapter comes from Eugen Herrigel's famous book *Zen in the Art of Archery* and shows not only how Zen has influenced martial arts such as Japanese archery, but how such martial arts themselves (in this case archery) become forms of Zen and of meditational practice, training and discipline, expressing the same nuances, meanings and simplicities as Zen.

Reading No. 16
From the Lotus Sutra

The Revelation of the Mahāyāna

The dull, who delight in petty rules,
Who are greedily attached to mortality,
Who have not, under countless Buddhas,
Walked the profound and mystic Way,
Who are harassed by all the sufferings -
To these I [at first] preach Nirvāna.
Such is the expedient I employ
To lead them to Buddha-wisdom.
Not yet could I say to them,
'You all shall attain to Buddhahood',
For the time had not yet arrived.
But now the very time has come
And I must preach the Great Vehicle...

The Buddha appears in the world
Only for this One Reality,
The other two not being real;
For never by a smaller Vehicle (Hinayāna)
[Could a Buddha] save any creature.
The Buddha himself is in the Great Vehicle (Mahāyāna)
And accordant with the Truth he has attained,
Enriched by meditation, and wisdom,
By it he saves all creatures.
I, having proved the Supreme Way,
The universality of the Great Vehicle,
If, by a Small Vehicle, I converted
Were it but one human being,
I should fall into grudging selfishness,
A thing that cannot be.
If men turn in faith to the Buddha,
The Tathāgata will not deceive them,
Having no selfish, envious desires,
Being free from all sins of the Law.

Hence, the Buddha, in the universe,
Is the One being perfectly fearless...

Know, O Shāriputra!
Of yore I made a vow,
In desire to cause all creatures,
To rank equally with me...

Whene'er I meet any of the living
I teach them the Buddha-Way;
The unwise remain confused
And, deluded, accept not my teaching...

I know that all these creatures
Have failed in previous lives,
Are firmly attached to base desires
And, infatuated, are in trouble...

They suffer the utmost misery.
Received into the womb in embryo,
They pass from generation to generation,
Poor in virtue and of little happiness,
Oppressed by all the sorrows
And dwelling in the thickets of debate,
Such as, Existence? or Non-existence?
Relying on their propositions,
Sixty-two in number,
They became rooted in false philosophy,
Tenacious and unyielding,
Self-sufficient and self-inflated,
Suspicious, warped, without faith.
During thousands and milliards of kalpas
Such hear not the name of Buddha,
Nor ever learn of the Truth;
These men are hard to save.
For this reason, Shāriputra,
I set up an expedient for them,
Proclaiming a Way to end suffering,
Revealing it as Nirvāna.
Yet, though I proclaim Nirvāna,
It is not real extinction;
All things from the beginning
Are ever of Nirvāna nature.
When a Buddha-son fulfils [his] course,
In the world to come he becomes Buddha.

It is because of my adaptability
That I tell of a Three-Vehicle Law,
[But truly] the World-honoured Ones
Preach the One-Vehicle Way.

Reading No. 17
Shingon Buddhist mandalas
By FINN STEFÁNSSON

In Shingon Buddhism two mandalas (In Japanese *mandara*) are central symbols of rituals and meditation. Each is a pictorial representation of the psycho-physical universe, a projection of the inner life. Each also represents the outflowing of Enlightenment to penetrate every sphere of phenomenal existence.

The photo shows the mandala which in Sanskrit is called the *Garbhakosadhatu Mandala* and in Japanese *Taizokai Mandara*, which means the 'womb-realm' mandala. The mandala represents Mahavairocana (Dainichi the Sun Buddha) as the body of Principle as-it-is or as it exists in the totality of phenomenal existence. It symbolises the unfolding compassion, growth and potentiality of the world of Enlightenment. Every sentient being is believed to have an inherent potentiality or seed (Buddha nature) that can be nourished in this womb of compassion to attain Enlightenment.

The mandala depicts 414 deities. In the centre, in the shape of an eight-petalled lotus, Mahavairocana the Sun Buddha sits, surrounded by four Buddhas and four bodhisattvas, symbolising the nine consciousnesses (of Buddhism). Among the Buddhas, who control virtues and effectiveness, there is Amida; among the bodhisattvas, who represent the vow to aid sentient beings, there is Avalokitesvara (Kannon). The centre as a whole symbolises the eternal process of seeking Enlightenment. The lotus symbolises the physical organ of the human heart, and thus this section can be considered to be representative of the attainment of Enlightenment within the physical body (*sokushinjobutsu*, see next text).

Garbhakosadhatu Mandala

Around the centre there are other reincarnations of Mahavairocana, 11 groups divided into the four corners of the world. To the north, that is the left, there is a group of Kannon and Jizo deities. The outer border of the mandala contains a total of 205 bodhisattvas, all representing manifestations of Mahavairocana as he infinitely creates the universe.

•   •   •

The other Shingon mandala, *Vajra-dhatu mandala* (In Japanese *Kongokai Mandara*, the 'diamond realm'), has 1461 deities in 9 sections. The *vajra* (diamond or thunderbolt) symbolises the power to penetrate ignorance and achieve integration. It deals primarily with the spiritual practice that leads to Enlightenment. The two mandalas, the womb and the diamond, operate together, the former symbolising the potentiality of Enlightenment and the latter the unchanging powers to achieve it.

Shingon is an esoteric form of Buddhism. When a master initiates his disciple into the doctrine, the *kanjo* ritual is used permitting the disciple to learn the *Taizo-kai* and *Kongokai* doctrines. The term *kanjo* in Japanese literally means 'aspersion with water'. Before the actual ceremony is performed, the initiate makes a series of vows, usually in the morning. Then early and late at night, the mandala doctrines are imparted ritually.

At these ceremonies the initiate is blind-folded with a red or white cloth and led to the mandala altar where he throws a flower to determine the Buddha or other deity to henceforth venerate, and is instructed in the appropriate *mantra* (words of power) and *mudra* (symbolic gestures) relating to the deity. He then is conducted through further symbolic rites and finally is sprinkled with holy water from five vessels, symbolising the five wisdoms of the Buddha, at which time sacred formulas are recited.

Reading No. 18

Sokushinjobutsu: 'Becoming a Buddha in this lifetime'

From the legend of Kukai

Sokushinjobutsu - the word means that people can attain Buddha-hood in their lifetime. The human self becomes Buddha. In other words, man is capable of demonstrating what Buddha means with his own body.

Sokushinjobutsu thus means to become Buddha as you are. Only Shingon has this doctrine. It is to be understood that body, soul and language become one with Buddha. Through this transformation, three holy functions arise. These three holy functions are shaped by '*shin*' in the word *sokushinjobutsu*. The word '*shin*' here means the living body or life. So the expression *sokushinjobutsu* means that the religion touches us in our real life, in our lifetime.

In the Heian period, besides the six Buddhist sects stemming from the Nara period, there were two more. These were Tendai

Buddhism, founded by the great master, Dengyo, on Mount Hiei at Kyoto, and Shingon Buddhism, founded by the Master (Kukai).

At that time Shingon and Tendai were new religions in Japan. Both founders had attended Chinese monasteries to study their doctrines before bringing them back to Japan.

Both these religions are fundamental for later Buddhism in Japan. The structures in these two forms of Buddhism can be found in the various forms of Buddhist faith which have so far developed in Japan.

In 812 A.D. Emperor Saga called in the most important monks from all the eight Buddhist sects to his palace to be informed about the fundamentals of their teachings.

Most of the monks explained the philosophical aspects of Buddhism. Not until the passing of a large number of lives could man hope to attain Buddha-hood, they taught.

But the Master (Kukai) expressed thus: 'First, man has to know his own mind. To know one's own mind to its depths is to know Buddha's mind. The one who knows Buddha's mind, can also learn to know the mind of mankind. The one who knows the truth in this world and becomes one with it may become Buddha while alive. He can become Buddha the way he is. Because then Buddha's body, words and mind become one with that person's body, words and mind.'

Thus, based on the holy writings of Buddhism, the Master taught that the one who seeks the wisdom of Buddha may realise his Buddha-nature by becoming one with Buddha's mind in the body he got from his father and mother.

The learned dignitaries, however, doubted the teachings they heard for the first time then. But the Master held his hands in the right position, recited the holy words and let his mind enter Buddha. That moment he demonstrated with his own body *sokushinjobutsu*. It is this state that the Dainichi Sutra teaches, in which man becomes totally one with the holy law. This state is called *gasokudainichi*.

At that moment the body was transformed into a golden Dainichi-Buddha. Sparkling light shone from it. The pillow he sat on became an eight-leaved lotus. All the monks present bowed down in wonder and admiration.

Our Master then demonstrated a doctrine which we can study closer in his treatise, *Sokushinjobutsu-gi*. This treatise explains the sublime teachings of the Shingon sect. It also shows the true value of the teachings for human beings and prepares the way for true religion.

Reading No. 19

Portrait of Kobo Daishi

[According to the explanation, the portrait was reproduced as part of the commemoration activities on the 1150th anniversary of the death of Kukai (Kobo Daishi). The portrait and its accompanying explanation come from the main temple of the Shingon sect at Koyasan. Copies of the portrait are sold to people who make votive offerings at the temple.]

Shinnyohoshino, one of Kobo Daishi's disciples, painted the portrait, but it is believed that Kobo Daishi completed it personally. On the left side of the portrait is the inscription *Namu daishi henjo kongo*. This is an invocation to Kobo Daishi honouring him as the power that enlightens the universe, and is used by people when they wish to call for his help and mercy.

On his deathbed Kobo Daishi made seven vows to his disciples, and one of them was:

'Even though you cannot see me you will nourish correct thoughts when you contemplate my portrait. When you listen to my teachings and seek refuge in my words I will look after you with great mercy.'

When one recites the phrase *Namu daishi henjo kongo* in front of the portrait one worships Kobo Daishi and invokes his power.

Reading No. 20
Honen's last testament

The method of final salvation that I have propounded is neither a sort of meditation, such as has been practised by many scholars in China and Japan, nor is it a repetition of the Buddha's name by those who have studied and understood the deep meaning of it. It is nothing but the mere repetition of the *'Namu Amida Butsu'*, without a doubt of His mercy, whereby one may be born into the Land of Perfect Bliss. The mere repetition with firm faith includes all the practical details, such as the three-fold preparation of mind and the four practical rules. If I as an individual had any doctrine more profound than this, I should miss the mercy of the two Honourable Ones, Amida and Shāka, and be left out of the Vow of the Amida Buddha. Those who believe this, though they clearly understand all the teachings Shāka taught throughout his whole life, should behave themselves like simple-minded folk, who know not a single letter, or like ignorant nuns or monks whose faith is implicitly simple. Thus without pedantic airs, they should fervently practise the repetition of the name of Amida, and that alone.

Reading No. 21
Nichiren's teaching

JAPAN AS THE CENTRE OF BUDDHISM'S REGENERATION

When, at a certain future time, the union of the state law and the Buddhist Truth shall be established, and the harmony between the two completed, both sovereign and subjects will faithfully adhere to the Great Mysteries. Then the golden age, such as were the ages under the reign of the sage kings of old, will be realised in these days of degeneration and corruption, in the time of the Latter Law.

Then the establishment of the Holy See will be completed, by imperial grant and the edict of the Dictator, at a spot comparable in its excellence with the Paradise of Vulture Peak. We have only to wait for the coming of the time. Then the moral law (*kaiho*) will be achieved in the actual life of mankind. The Holy See will then be the seat where all men of the three countries [India, China and Japan] and the whole Jambudvīpa [world] will be initiated into the mysteries of confession and expiation; and even the great deities, Brahmā and Indra, will come down into the sanctuary and participate in the initiation.

NICHIREN AS A PROPHET

The Lord Shākya proclaimed to all celestial beings that when, in the fifth five hundred years after his death, all the truths of Buddhism should be shrouded in darkness, the Bodhisattva of Superb Action (Vishishtahāritra) should be commissioned to save the most wicked of men who were degrading the truth, curing the hopeless lepers by the mysterious medicine of the Adoration of the Lotus of the Perfect Truth. Can this proclamation be a falsehood? If this promise be not vain, how can the rulers of the people of Japan remain in safety, who, being plunged in the whirlpool of strife and malice, have rebuked, reviled, struck and banished the messenger of the Tathāgata and his followers commissioned by Buddha to propagate the Lotus of Truth?

When they hear me say this, people will say that it is a curse; yet, those who propagate the Lotus of Truth are indeed the parents of all men living in Japan.... I, Nichiren, am the master and lord of the sovereign, as well as of all the Buddhists of other schools. Notwithstanding this, the rulers and the people treat us thus maliciously. How should the sun and the moon bless them by giving them light? Why should the earth not refuse to let them abide upon it?.... Therefore, also, the Mongols are coming to chastise them. Even if all the soldiers from the five parts of India were called together, and the mountain of the Iron Wheel (Chakravāla) were fortified, how could they succeed in repelling the invasion? It is decreed that all the inhabitants of Japan shall suffer from the invaders. Whether this comes to pass or not will prove whether or not Nichiren is the real propagator of the Lotus of Truth.

Reading No. 22

The Ox-herding pictures

By AAGE MARCUS

The new attitude towards life in Zen, which first and foremost is built on the basis of helping others, was in a very special way expressed in a series of pictures. By the twelfth century Zen art had created a series of 10 pictures as guides to Zen teaching and meditation. These are the famous Ox-herding pictures. The form in which they are reproduced here is due to the Japanese Zen artist, Shubun, who lived in the fifteenth century, but the series goes back to older models. Since then they have been copied countlessly in China as well as in Japan, and in the Far East they are comparable to popular devotional pictures and legends of saints within the Catholic church.

Brief commentaries have been added to the pictures from time immemorial, partly in poetry and partly in prose. The interpretation they offer in lyrical terms can be summarised thus: The first picture shows man in the shape of a herdsman looking for the ox which is a symbol of divinity or the special meaning of life which can be obtained through Zen. In the second picture the herdsman has been taught Zen and knows in what direction to seek the ox. He has even found the tracks of the heavenly ox. In the third picture he himself sees the ox and in the fourth he fights hard to possess it. He succeeds and in the fifth picture he takes it home and masters it so much that in the sixth picture he can casually ride it the last part of the way while playing a flute. In the seventh picture he has come home and *the ox is forgotten*, that is, the dualism or gap between the divine and man is overcome.

But it is possible to attain an even higher understanding, as is suggested in the eighth picture which is completely empty. Indeed, in reality this is the only way in which the experience of the mystic can be presented. Still, the following two pictures are the most important to an understanding of Zen. The ninth, called 'back to the origin, to the sources', only shows some rocks and a blooming tree by the water: this is 'nature', pure and undisturbed by man and his problems, and in the tenth picture the *new* man is to be seen: the herdsman, who has found, caught and tamed the ox, forgotten

9   10

it and himself, now goes out into the world with his great inalienable understanding to help others and maybe lead them to the tracks of 'the ox'.

That this is not a monastic or especially ascetic aspect of the world which appears here, but is in fact the world in all its worldliness is illustrated by the jovial and not very ceremonious person - a symbolic figure - who is depicted together with the herdsman.

Reading No. 23
An ordinary day in the Zen temple of Daishuin

By POUL ERIK PILMANN

Daishuin is a small Rinzai Zen temple on the banks of the Oshidori river at Ryoanji in Kyoto. There the Zen master, Morinaga Roshi, and four monks and eleven novices live. The monks are the disciples of the master and they have placed their lives in his hands, whereas the novices only have bound themselves to live in the temple for a certain period.

Every day in Daishuin is like any other. The practical life is carefully planned, often into single movements, and this gives the monks an unlimited freedom to devote to every single act their whole attention. This is what life is about in the temple.

At four o'clock a.m. you fold your sleeping pad into a pillow, dress and go to the *hondo* (main hall). Here the Zen master conducts the recitation of sutras in the first hours of the day. The monks are on their knees, do not move, but recite the Buddhist doctrines in one voice to the rhythm of quick strokes of a bell.

Zazen (seated meditation) begins at five o'clock. Back in the *zendo* (meditation hall) the monks sit in the lotus position and for an hour-and-a-half they concentrate entirely on respiration, breathing in and out. After long practice the body and the mind become tranquil and breathing reaches its slowest possible rhythm. In this condition it may happen that the monks doze off, and to counteract this sleepiness they can signal with a movement of their hands for the superior monk to give them four blows with a stick across their shoulders. In this way they keep wide awake during *zazen*, and this is crucial.

At seven breakfast is served. You kneel in silence during the meal. In the temple you do one thing at a time. When you talk you talk, and when you eat, you eat. Each monk has three bowls which fit into one another. In the first he gets rice gruel, in the second cabbage soup and in the smallest fresh or pickled vegetables. The food is handed round three times in a very special way, you fold your hands in front of you if you want more, and you bend down when you have got enough. After the meal all get a little warm water in the biggest bowl and in this the other bowls and chopsticks are washed. The last bits of food are swallowed with the water, because in the temple not a rice corn is wasted and not a drop of water.

After breakfast all meet to perform the tea ceremony with the Zen master. The ceremonial green tea is prepared and served by Nin-san, who has specially learned the difficult art which can be the aim of a life-long study. Nin-san performs the serving of tea in one long movement, almost gliding, which does not stop until the cups are collected, washed and put on a shelf. On this occasion the Zen master turns to some of the monks or novices if he feels they need his advice or help....

For the rest of the morning all the monks perform their part in doing the necessary work of the temple. This is often hard manual labour and this physical activity is the natural opposite of *zazen*.

The understanding obtained in *zazen* disappears if it is not expressed in practical life, just as the meaning of daily labour disappears if you cannot express yourself.

The Zen master Pai-chang (720-814) who founded the meditation hall tradition pronounced it directly and without any fuss in the first rule of monastic life: a day without work is a day without food.

The main meal of the day is at midday. Instead of rice gruel

Zen Buddhist students practise *zazen* at all times of the day and night both indoors and outdoors

boiled rice is served, otherwise the food is the same as in the morning. It may seem monotonous to the outsider, but the meals are nutritionally well balanced and tasty, because they are prepared with the greatest care and with respect for the raw materials available.

When all have finished the senior monk shares out the work which lies outside the daily programme. During this he surrenders to his great weakness: he loves to tease. Once he asked San-san if he had remembered to water the tomato plants. For San-san is very jealous of his honour and work, and he never forgets to water the tomato plants. San-san laughed and rocked his head because he is also very good-natured and answered that the tomato plants would soon outgrow the senior monk.

At five o'clock it is time to take a bath. The monastic rules prescribe that the monks shall keep their bodies and minds free of impurity, and keeping this in mind they shall wash off dirt from the body and the mind in a process as close as the meeting of water and skin.

After the washing off they quietly glide down in the common baths which Do-san has heated by means of scrap wood and fallen

113

leaves with such attention that the water reaches its ideal temperature the moment the last twigs stop burning, and with the same concentration the monks try to experience the water as water and not only as something pleasantly hot and fluid.

The evening meal is very light and consists mainly of the left-overs from the dinner. Many of the monks hardly touch the food because it is best not to have a full stomach when the evening *zazen* begins.

At seven *zazen* begins. Back in the *zendo* the monks take up the lotus position and for two hours they concentrate all their attention on their respiration. Breathing in and out. Very, very slowly and without any effort they breathe down air through the nasal cavity to the bottom of the abdominal cavity and let it flow back even more slowly through the body and out of the nasal cavity.

One evening the Zen master told me: 'When you breathe in you take in all the universe, and when you breathe out breathe out all the universe. You are not alone'.

At half past nine the monks fold out their *zazen* pillows so they become bedclothing, undress and go to sleep.

*   *   *

After reading this description of life at Daishuin the sceptical reader will perhaps think that Zen training is a rigid blend of asceticism and masochism. My experience of life at Daishuin is totally different. The monks in the temple are not in the process of expiating sin or worrying themselves to death. On the contrary they are working on a Zen Buddhist theological education which in a surprisingly short time gives them a conspicuous physical and psychical well-being which most clearly is expressed in a strong independence of manner and a spontaneously affectionate and creative personality.

The theological education continues in a Zen monastery where discipline is far stronger than in the temple, and which is called by some the spiritual hothouse of Zen Buddhism. Ultimately the education leads to the attainment of total consciousness. As a rule Zen masters leave it to less enlightened people to confuse the issue by describing this consciousness. It is not without cause that books and writing tools are banned in a Zen monastery. Compared to what 20 minutes of *zazen* every morning does to enlighten the issue, reading about Zen is of very little use.

Or as a Zen master once said: 'The finger pointing at the moon must not be mistaken for the moon itself'.

Reading No. 24

Zazen: sitting meditation for beginners

By POUL ERIK PILMANN

How to sit is very important for *zazen*. The correct sitting posture is achieved by sitting down (in loose-fitting clothes on a hard pillow) with crossed legs so that your right foot rests on your left thigh and your left foot on your right thigh. Obviously, at the beginning this can be difficult for some people. It is best to train one leg at a time, i.e. left foot on your right thigh and right foot under your left thigh or vice versa. The spine must be vertical, your ears in line with your shoulders and your nose in line with your navel.

Relax your shoulders by letting your arms dangle down and back, lift the back of your head and pull in your chin a bit. Push your buttocks back as far as possible and distribute your weight between

Interior of the *zazen* hall

them and your knees. Now gather your hands in your lap by seizing your left hand thumb with your right hand and place the rest of the fingers of your left hand over those of your right hand so that the thumbs are hidden in the hollow of your hand.

Let your tongue rest gently against the palate and set your teeth without biting them together. Lower your eyes so you look about one metre ahead of you, but keep your eyes open at all times. Stay wide awake and sit absolutely still.

Now *zazen* can begin. The inner balance between relaxation and concentration occurs as you consciously experience and control inhalation and exhalation.

It is extremely important that you breathe with your diaphragm and breathe out fully, but otherwise let your breathing find its own natural rhythm. Initially, you will find that it is difficult to concentrate so much on your breathing. All sorts of thoughts will cross your mind but you must not try to stop them - just let them pass through without taking any notice. Moreover, you will probably get pains in your back and in your knee joints but they will disappear gradually as your training proceeds.

It is absolutely essential that you meditate regularly, at least 20 minutes at a time and preferably every morning or if convenient every evening when the house is silent.

If at a later date, after you have achieved consistency in your training, including a good sitting position, and you wish to expand your Zen skills to incorporate working with *koan* and somewhat longer periods of meditation, be sure to obtain personal instruction from a competent master.

Reading No. 25
Ten haiku

(1)
A day of quiet gladness, -
Mount Fuji is veiled
In misty rain

(2)
The temple bell dies away.
The scent of flowers in the evening
Is still tolling the bell.

(3)
A Rose of Sharon
By the roadside;
The horse has eaten it.

(4)
The old pond:
A frog jumps in,
The sound of the water.

(5)
The butterfly
Resting upon the temple bell,
Asleep.

(6)
The cow comes
Moo! Moo!
Out of the mist.

(7)
A swallow
Flew out of the nose
Of the Great Buddha.

(8)
On the temple bell,
Glowing,
A firefly.

(9)
A stray cat
Excreting
In the winter garden.

(10)
The straight hole
Made by pissing
In the snow outside the door.

The parody of Basho's 'Old Pond' in the illustration runs like this
(said by the frog):
'If there were a pond (around here) I would jump in, and let Basho
hear (the plop)!

Reading No. 26

The Garden of Emptiness - the rock garden at Ryoanji

By FINN STEFÁNSSON

The stone garden at Ryoanji (The Dragon Peace Temple) in Kyoto is in all its simplicity the best known Zen garden in Japan. It is primarily an object of meditation. The garden itself consists of a rectangle of 23 by 9 metres of carefully raked white pebbles and 15 rocks placed in groups of odd numbers. Three of the sides have roofed walls, mainly of the colour ochre. Thus the verandah of the temple (*jojo*) is the only place from which the garden can be viewed.

According to tradition the garden was created by the great artist Soami (d. 1525). Most of these garden artists were at the same time Zen monks.

There are many interpretations of the stone garden. Does it symbolise a group of rocks in a huge ocean, perhaps Japan? Are they mountains penetrating the clouds? Is the wall a frame and the

Riyonanji Temple garden, Kyoto

garden a picture? Should the garden be understood as the meeting between the movable and the immovable as in *haiku* poems? At least the interpretation has nothing to do with the impermanence of life, because in this garden no flowers or leaves wither and it is not dependent on transient momentary beauty.

The garden is called *mutei* (the garden of nothingness) or *kutai*(the garden of emptiness). Emptiness understood as the empty space in pictorial art, stillness in music, the ultra-brief form in lyrics, non-movement in a dance - all these are aesthetical-religious aspects exploited with great sophistication in Japanese art.

To understand emptiness - the formless, the opposite of diversity and peculiarity - one must have a form. Emptiness and stillness are only experienced paradoxically when they are broken: the splash of a frog in the still pond. Emptiness or the absolute is the end goal of meditation and it annihilates everything else as 'mere' interpretation. The paradox can be put this way: we experience emptiness as form and form as emptiness.

Reading No. 27
Zen in the Art of Archery

By EUGEN HERRIGEL

'You have described only too well', replied the Master, 'where the difficulty lies. Do you know why you cannot wait for the shot and why you get out of breath before it has come? The right shot at the right moment does not come because you do not let go of yourself. You do not wait for fulfilment, but brace yourself for failure. So long as that is so, you have no choice but to call forth something yourself that ought to happen independently of you, and so long as you call it forth your hand will not open in the right way - like the hand of a child: it does not burst open like the skin of a ripe fruit.'

I had to admit to the Master that this interpretation made me more confused than ever. 'For ultimately', I said, 'I draw the bow and loose the shot in order to hit the target. The drawing is thus a means to an end, and I cannot lose sight of this connection. The child knows nothing of this, but for me the two things cannot be disconnected.'

'The right art', cried the Master, 'is purposeless, aimless! The more obstinately you try to learn how to shoot the arrow for the sake of hitting the goal, the less you will succeed in the one and the further the other will recede. What stands in your way is that you have a much too wilful will. You think that what you do not do yourself does not happen.'

'But you yourself have told me often enough that archery is not a pastime, not a purposeless game, but a matter of life and death!'

'I stand by that. We master archers say: one shot - one life! What this means, you cannot yet understand. But perhaps another image will help you, which expresses the same experience. We master archers say: with the upper end of the bow the archer pierces the sky, on the lower end, as though attached by a thread, hangs the earth. If the shot is loosed with a jerk there is a danger of the thread snapping. For purposeful and violent people the rift becomes final, and they are left in the awful centre between heaven and earth.'

'What must I do, then?' I asked thoughtfully.

'You must learn to wait properly.'

'And how does one learn that?'

'By letting go of yourself, leaving yourself and everything yours behind you so decisively that nothing more is left of you but a purposeless tension.'

'So I must become purposeless - on purpose?' I heard myself say.

'No pupil has ever asked me that, so I don't know the right answer.'

'And when do we begin these new exercises?'

'Wait until it is time.'

* * *

'Do you now understand', the Master asked me one day after a particularly good shot, 'what I mean by "It shoots", "It hits"?'

'I'm afraid I don't understand anything more at all', I answered, 'even the simplest things have got in a muddle. Is it "I" who draws the bow, or is it the bow that draws me into the state of highest tension? Do "I" hit the goal, or does the goal hit me? Is "It" spiritual when seen by the eyes of the body, and corporeal when seen by the eyes of the spirit - or both or neither? Bow, arrow, goal and an ego, all melt into one another, so that I can no longer separate them. And even the need to separate has gone. For as soon as I take the bow and shoot, everything becomes so clear and straightforward and so ridiculously simple....'

'Now at last', the Master broke in, 'the bowstring has cut right through you.'

6

The New Religions
of Japan

Since the mid-nineteenth century, many of Japan's religious movements have developed separately from and independent of the
main religious traditions of Shinto and Buddhism. These movements
are generally known as the new religions. Although the oldest of
them, such as Tenrikyo, are around 150 years old, they are still
relatively new as religions when compared to Shinto or Buddhism,
which in Japan are some 1400 years old. The new religions are also
'new' because they have offered new opportunities for religious
expression and understanding in the modern world, thus presenting
a new alternative to the older religious traditions.

There are large numbers of new religions in Japan, with many
hundreds of them currently active and many other new groups
appearing all the time. Obviously, it is not possible here to discuss
all of their characteristics separately. Generally speaking, however,
the new religions do have many things in common with each other,
and in this chapter we shall examine these common characteristics.
From the readings we shall also learn something of the specific
nature and aspects of a number of new religions.

Historically speaking, new religions began appearing in Japan
from around the middle of the nineteenth century onwards
Although the earliest new religions such as Tenrikyo grew largely
in rural areas, these days they are more commonly associated with
the towns and cities. Certainly, those that have appeared during
the twentieth century (such as Soka Gakkai, Rissho Kosei-kai and

Mahikari, all of which are represented in the readings) have flourished especially in the cities, which have been the areas that have undergone most change and upheaval over the years.

Generally, the new religions have been syncretic: that is to say, they have assimilated many themes and ideas from various other religious traditions. This borrowing has mostly been from Shinto, Buddhism and the folk religious tradition, but some have incorporated ideas also from Christianity, such as the idea of a Supreme God. Many of these syncretic elements will become clear during the readings, when many of the characteristics found in the world of Japanese religions, for example the importance of purification and the role of the ancestors, will be observed in the new religions.

Most Japanese new religions have developed around a powerful individual leader who believes him or herself to have received a special revelation from a god or to have found a special message of truth within the Buddhist scriptures. Often such leaders are believed, by their followers, to possess special powers and to be able to communicate directly with the world of the spirits for the benefit of their followers. In many new religions, also, the leaders are believed to be able to heal illnesses and to pacify unhappy spirits who are afflicting people.

In addition, the new religions provide for their members a way of living and an individual means of dealing with their lives and problems, and with the search for happiness, based on religious practice, prayer and discipline. They also provide the means whereby people may be able to confront in some form or other personal problems and crises, either through group therapy sessions, through meetings with trained religious counsellors or through religious rituals. In doing this the new religions invariably preach an optimistic message, teaching that all problems can be solved, and that life on earth is meant to be happy and joyous.

Reading what the Japanese new religions say to their followers and to the outside world gives us an idea of the nature of these modern religious movements as they operate in Japan at present.

AN OUTLINE OF THE READINGS

Five readings (Nos. 28 to 32) centre on **Tenrikyo**, one of the oldest and largest of the new religions which has been selected to provide a representative example of a new religion. Like all the new religions, Tenrikyo has drawn influences from many religious traditions, but it displays many distinctly Shinto themes. It has its own creation myths (Reading No. 28, taken from the writings of Tenrikyo's foundress Nakayama Miki) which show many similarities with the

Mother church at Tenri

Shinto myths recounted in Chapter Four. Tenrikyo, however, has its own deity, God the Parent, who is seen as the source of the Shinto deities, and Reading No. 28 starts with God the parent teaching Izanami and Izanagi how to create humans.

Like many new religions, Tenrikyo owes its origins and inspiration to an inspired founding figure who receives a message from the divine world, and Reading No. 29 introduces us to the story of Nakayama Miki, the peasant woman who is revered as the foundress of Tenrikyo, and the way in which she first encountered God the Parent. It is interesting to note that these revelations came to her during religious rituals aimed at solving family problems connected to illness.

The solution of problems of the sort outlined here, such as illness and personal misfortune, is itself one of the main activities of the new religions, and the desire to seek help in the face of such problems is an important factor in drawing people into the new religions. As this reading shows, similar factors are often at work in the lives of the founders of new religions, many of whom are drawn by misfortunes in their own (or their families') lives into religious activities that bring them into contact with the divine, give them insights into the truth and provide them with revelations which lead them to form their own religions.

Most new religions develop their own holy centres, usually at the place where their founder or foundress was born or received their revelations. Tenrikyo is perhaps unique in creating a city (Tenri City) around its holy centre where Nakayama Miki lived and taught, and where it considers that God the Parent first gave life to mankind. Reading No. 30 comes from a brochure given out to visitors to Tenrikyo's headquarters at Tenri, and introduces us both to the holy centre and to some of the religion's basic doctrines, such as the importance of living a joyous life and of helping others so that all may benefit from the grace of God the Parent and be happy.

The last two readings from Tenrikyo introduce us to another important theme in the new religions: their role in explaining why misfortunes occur, and the ways in which they deal with problems such as illness and other such practical problems in the lives of their followers. Reading No. 31 presents Tenrikyo's explanation of illness which states that physical problems originate in the mind and that moral misdeeds (for example, anger, hatred and avarice) are root causes of personal problems such as illness.

Tenrikyo's teaching that illness is not just something requiring medical treatment but also spiritual action is commonly found in the new religions. Illness in such terms is seen as a warning light teaching one to reform one's life, to devote more attention to spiritual practices, and to try to lead a more morally disciplined life. Tenrikyo thus teaches the importance of gratitude in all things, for illness itself is interpreted as a blessing from God, a sign that one's life has got out of balance and needs reform. Reading No. 32 expands on this by showing the role of a Tenrikyo counsellor in helping people solve practical problems in their lives, and provides the sort of incident commonly found in the new religions: an apparently miraculous happening or change of circumstance that results from people taking heed of the teachings of the religion.

Personal religious practice, often of an ascetic nature, is very important in all the new religions, and the next three readings (Nos. 33-35), which look at a very small but well-known religion, **Itto-en**, bring this out. Itto-en's 300 members live together as one large family in a communal and ascetic lifestyle. Reading No. 33 gives one of Itto-en's main prayers, which outlines the importance of service to others, while No. 34 introduces us to Itto-en's founder, his philosophy, and the Itto-en ideal of owning nothing. The last reading on Itto-en, No. 35, further deals with the importance of service to others and discusses Itto-en's communal lifestyle in which individual members have no personal possessions.

Two new religions both with their roots in the Nichiren Buddhist tradition form the focus of the next readings. **Soka Gakkai** is the biggest of the new religions of Japan and the one with the largest following overseas, having several thousand members in the USA and a growing presence in the UK and other parts of Europe.

Soka Gakkai developed as a lay organisation affiliated to the Nichiren Shoshu Buddhist sect, but since a bitter dispute arose between its leaders and the Buddhist hierarchy of Nichiren Shoshu in 1990 it has become independent. Its aggressive proselytism, especially in the 1950s and 1960s, its seeming intolerance of other religions, and its political ambitions of uniting religion and state under its guidance, which led it to form the Komeito or 'Clean Government Party', aroused much hostility in Japan especially in the 1950s and 1960s. Since then, partly due to the problematic relationship of religion and politics in Japan (see Chapter 8), it has severed its official links with Komeito. It has also become less overtly militant, shifting its focus from explicit goals of world conversion, to more idealised statements about its commitment to universal peace and harmony.

Soka Gakkai displays a common Japanese religious notion that practical benefits come from religious involvement, and asserts that individual benefits and happiness result from practising its faith. Though it has been criticised for its apparent materialism in this, its members frequently testify to the practical as well as spiritual results that they feel come from their faith. The religion also sets as its goal the establishment of universal harmony and world peace, and works hard to further this through its peace foundations and educational activities. However, harmony has its limits, for Soka Gakkai considers that true peace is only attainable through world conversion to its teachings, and it rarely cooperates or works with other religious groups or peace movements to these ends. The Readings illustrate the different faces of the religion over the years: Reading 36, with its talk of direct benefits and of militant conversion shows its public orientation in the 1960s, while Reading 37 (produced in 1992 after the split with Nichiren Shoshu) exhibits its more gentle contemporary public posture.

Another new religion with its roots in Nichiren Buddhism is **Rissho Kosei-kai**, which is the focus of Readings Nos. 38 and 39. Both highlight issues of importance in the new religions in general, the first dealing with the importance of personal worship, and the second with the provision of guidance and help in dealing with personal and everyday problems. In Rissho Kosei-kai members discuss their problems and feelings in groups known as *hoza*, and this reading describes the aims and dynamics of this form of group therapy and counselling.

The next two readings, Nos. 40 and 41, look at the new religion **Seicho-no-Ie** and provide examples of the syncretic nature of many new religions. In these two readings taken from Seicho-no-Ie literature and brochures, aspects of Christian and Buddhist thought are clearly manifest. A further theme common in most new religions and strongly expressed in these two texts is the view that the religion has a special mission to save humanity and lead it to the truth, harmony and peace.

The final reading in this chapter, No. 42, comes from **Mahikari**, a new religion that has become especially popular in the last few years because of its spiritual healing practices. The central practice of Mahikari is known as *Mahikari no waza* or *tekazashi*. This is a technique of purification and exorcism in which members of the religion are believed to radiate, through their hands, a beam of pure light that comes from Su-God, the great deity of Mahikari, and is transmitted to them through a holy amulet that they receive on joining Mahikari.

The word Mahikari itself means 'pure light', and members believe that the light that is radiated during *Mahikari no waza* will purify all those who receive it. As a result they will be cured of diseases, spiritual problems, and other misfortunes. Mahikari believes that many of these problems are caused by evil or unhappy spirits of some sort or other, that possess and afflict the living. As Reading No. 42 makes clear, Mahikari's purification technique can solve the problems not only of the possessed but of the spirits that are troubling them as well.

The new religions of Japan continue to grow in numbers and in terms of followers. The extent of their growth especially in this century makes them one of the most dynamic and active aspects of religion in Japan. The readings in this chapter bring out the diversities to be found among the new religions, as well as illustrating many of the common elements to be found in them.

Underlying all of these themes is the ability of the new religions to speak to Japanese people on a level that they can readily understand, and to provide them with teachings and religious techniques that enable them to deal with the problems they face in life and that help them live a better and happier life. This factor, which is shown especially in the readings dealing with Mahikari's *tekazashi* technique, Rissho Kose-kai's *hoza* groups, the aims of Soka Gakkai, and the counselling and spiritual guidance given in Tenrikyo, is probably the most constant element in the new religions, and serves as a major reason for their continued success in Japan today.

The Mahikari temple and headquarters

Performing spiritual purification according to the Mahikari practice

READINGS FROM TENRIKYO

Reading No. 28

From the *Ofudesaki* of Nakayama Miki

Ofudesaki, s. 146-152 (Part VI), Tenri 1983.

I, God the Parent, called forth both *Izanagi*
and *Izanami* and taught them the providence
how to create human beings.

Originally it was a muddy ocean and I
found therein a fish and a serpent. Drawing
them forth, I created the first husband
and wife.

The origin of this universe was a muddy
ocean, living therein were nothing but
a large number of loaches.

Among them I found a fish and a serpent.
And after gazing at them, I found that
they had the faces of human beings.

By seeing them, an idea came to no one but
the truly sincere mind of Tsukihi.

It should be good, if I call together instruments
to add to them, and teach them
My providence one by one.

These instruments were *Kunisazuchi* and
Tsukiyomi; if I put them into their bodies,

If I call *Kumoyomi*, *Kashikone*, *Ōtonobe*
and *Taishokuten* altogether,

Then after a counsel with them I, God,
came to the conclusion that the creation of
this world must be positively commenced.

Since then the providence of God has been
by no means easy.

It was indeed difficult, because I was beginning
things which had never existed
before.

I suppose that there is no one who knows
the truth of the creation of this world.

Henceforth I will tell you any and everything
one by one. Never take it to be
false!

I created human beings, taking a fish and
a serpent as seed and seedbed.

Entering into their bodies, Tsukihi taught
them the providence step by step.

The number of these children amounted
to nine hundred million, ninety-nine thousand,
nine hundred and ninety-nine.

It took three days and three nights to conceive
these children, and *Izanami* stayed
there for three years and three months.

The first born was five *bu*, (about half
an inch) tall, and grew up by five *bu*
repeatedly.

By this providence once taught, children
were conceived into the same womb three
times.

The true and real God of this universe is
Tsukihi. The others are all instruments.

To create human beings, I called together
these instruments, and gave a sacred name
to each of them.

Izanagi and *Izanami* are the names of the
prime providence in the creation. In relation
to this providence, the supreme god
of this country is enshrined and respected
in the Teishōkō-no-Daijingu.

Henceforward I will teach you step by step
any and everything of which you have
never heard.

Henceforth I will tell you exclusively about
the creation of human beings.

Reading No. 29
The Shrine of Tsukihi
[Excerpts]

'I am the Creator, the true and real God. There is preordination in this Residence. At this time I have descended here to save all mankind. I wish to receive Miki as the Shrine of God.'

With these words, spoken in a voice full of divine majesty, the whole house became permeated with spiritual presence. No one who was there dared to raise his head, neither Zenbei, head of the family, nor his relatives, nor even Ichibei, an ascetic monk. Indeed it was a god they had never heard of and a strange revelation they had never dreamed of. Zenbei did not understand the revelation at first, but upon reflection he realised that this revelation was truly a serious matter for the Nakayama family and was most unlikely to be accepted by them. While he was considering the matter in this way, he suddenly recalled a series of events that had occurred since the winter of the previous year.

It was on 26 October 1837 (Tenpo 8), when his eldest son, Shuji, seventeen, felt a sudden pain in his left leg while he was sowing barley in the fields, along with his mother, Miki. The pain was so severe that he was barely able to return home, using his rake as a crutch. A physician was consulted immediately, and though he did his utmost in treating the patient, applying a mentholated ointment, nothing seemed to ease the pain at all. At the suggestion of one of those present, Zenbei sent a messenger to Ichibei of Nagataki Village, who was locally renowned for his healing powers. However, Ichibei was away in Nigo Village at that time...

Then at ten o'clock on the evening of 23 October 1838 (Tenpo 9), in addition to Shuji's sore leg, Zenbei had trouble with his eyes, and Miki had a severe pain in Her back. Thus, there were now three ailing persons under one roof. It was during the Inoko Festival in Shoyashiki Village, and Ichibei happened to be there at his relatives, the Inui family. Zenbei sent a messenger for Ichibei, who came at once, saying, 'This must be serious. Let us hold an incantation'. Then he proceeded to prepare for the ritual. Scarcely waiting for daybreak, he sent a messenger for Soyo, who had regularly served as medium, but, unfortunately, she was not at home. Having no alternative, Ichibei requested that Miki take her place and bear the *gohei* as medium. Suddenly, in the midst of intent prayer, came the revelation through Her mouth:

'I wish to receive Miki as the Shrine of God.'

Miki had been sitting straight, night after day, for three consecutive days, holding the *gohei* in Her hands. She had taken neither meal nor rest during this time. Sometimes She would sit calmly, but at other times She would solemnly reveal the intention of the God of Origin in a resounding voice, Her hands trembling and wavering so violently that the paper fringes of the *gohei* were torn to shreds.

Those present still continued their talk to see if there were any possible means to persuade God to ascend. Naturally, they consulted Ichibei, but the matter had already proved to be beyond his powers. Even less could any of the others suggest an acceptable idea. Meanwhile, the strain and exhaustion on Miki, who was intently conveying the will of God day and night, taking neither food nor rest, increased visibly. Zenbei, fearing it might cost Her life if the situation continued, finally concluded that there was no alternative but to comply. At eight o'clock on the morning of the 26th, he accepted the will of God and declared with firm resolution:

'I offer Miki to You.'

At this, Miki's agitated behaviour became quiet for the first time in many hours, and at that instant Miki Nakayama was settled as the Shrine of God. The mind of God the Parent entered into Her, and She, revealing the divine will, began the ultimate teaching for saving all mankind. Indeed She is the One whom we revere as the Shrine of Tsukihi, the One whom we yearn after as the Parent of the Divine Model, and the One whom we glorify as Oyasama.

This event fell on 26 October 1838 (Tenpo 9), when Oyasama was in Her forty-first year.

> What I, Tsukihi, think now is spoken through Her
> mouth. Human is the mouth that speaks, but
> divine is the mind that thinks within.

> Listen attentively to Me! It is because I, Tsukihi,
> borrow Her mouth, while I, Tsukihi, lend My mind
> to Her.

Ofudesaki XII, 67, 68

The Life of Oyasama: Foundress of Tenrikyo, s. 1-7, (Tenri).

Reading No. 30

Oyasato: Tenrikyo's headquarters

Tenri City, where the Tenrikyo Church Headquarters is located, is a religious city that has expanded in direct proportion with the growth of Tenrikyo. The streets are crowded with people wearing black 'happi' jackets with white lettering on the back that spells out 'Tenrikyo'. The city is filled with a bright and lively atmosphere.

Visitors and those who meet them exchange greetings: 'Welcome home', and 'I'm home now'. These greetings sound strange to those who visit Tenri for the first time, but there is a deep religious meaning in them.

We are taught that God the Parent, Tenri-Ō-no-Mikoto, created human beings in order that He might share their joy by seeing them lead a joyous life. The Kanrodai now stands as a proof of human creation at the spot in the centre of the Main Sanctuary of the Tenrikyo Church Headquarters. This place, called the Jiba, is the birthplace of man and the source of human life.

At the Jiba, God the Parent, Tenri-Ō-no-Mikoto resides, and Oyasama, the Foundress, whom all the Tenrikyo followers adore as their beloved Parent, remains, in this Residence. Though She hid her physical being, She is always working for the salvation of mankind. This is why this place is called Oyasato (Parental Home).

Therefore, a pilgrimage to this place is commonly called a 'return to Jiba' or 'return to Oyasato' which means a return to the birthplace of mankind.

Furthermore, the Jiba is the place where the Service, the source of all salvation, is performed as the way to a joyous life, and where the *sazuke* (divine grant) is bestowed as a means to save people from illnesses.

Tenrikyo followers deepen their faith by returning to Oyasato and then with zealous faith go out to all corners of the world to engage enthusiastically in missionary work.

As an outward expression of their joy of faith the Oyasato construction is in progress with the goal of fulfilling the divine words '8-cho square (188 acres) is the Divine Residence'.

The Jiba, Oyasato, is truly the very core of the source of all salvation.

Most couples in Japan get married in a Shinto ceremony, which includes taking sips of saké

THE TEACHINGS OF TENRIKYO

Tenrikyo is a religion revealed by God the Parent Himself to save all the people in the world to lead a joyous life.

God the Parent is not only the original god who created human beings and the world in the beginning, but the true and real god who eternally gives life to all beings and constantly protects and cares for them.

However, man, being unaware of this truth, may mistakenly believe that he lives solely with his own power, and tends to be self-centred and endarken his own life which would otherwise be bright and promising.

God the Parent, who pitied this situation, revealed the whole truth about the creation and the ultimate teachings for joyous life through the Foundress Miki Nakayama as His Shrine at the original Residence (the Jiba) on 26 October 1838 as promised at the time of creation.

She not only conveyed the will of God the Parent by mouth and writings as God wished, but demonstrated the teachings of God the Parent in Her daily living. It is through the Foundress that human beings can learn the divine will and the goal of human life.

What sort of life then is a joyous life, the goal of all mankind? It is not just an idea or an ideal of life. It is a life filled with joy with all sicknesses, calamities, conflicts and various other forms of human sufferings resolved.

Joyous life is not just for one person. It should be enjoyed by all the people of the world, because we are taught that we are the children of God the Parent and so we are all brothers and sisters.

The Service and *sazuke* were taught as a means of attaining this goal.

Just as we are taught that 'the human body is a thing borrowed, the mind alone is ours', we are kept alive by borrowing our bodies according to the way we use our minds, which we are free to use as we please. It is therefore important that we use our minds towards a joyous life in accordance with God the Parent's will.

When we thus understand God the Parent's will and the fact that we are kept alive by the grace of God, our self-centred minds give way to a deep sense of gratitude for God's infinite blessings. We then feel like helping each other and saving other people. This is the true sincerity which God the Parent is seeking among men. The actions that result from such a feeling is called *hinokishin*.

The Tenrikyo faith teaches us to reform our minds in this manner and base our everyday lives on the teachings. It is not salvation just for oneself, or for prosperity and happiness just for oneself. It is to save all the people equally.

Today the teachings of God the Parent have spread not only in Japan, but also to various foreign countries. There are over 16,200 churches and over 2,000,000 followers. A steady advance is being made towards the world of joyous life.

Oyasato - brochure of Tenrikyo.

Reading No. 31

On medical care and the causes of illness

From a Tenrikyo brochure

A MESSAGE TO EVERYONE WHO IS ILL

A re you seeking self-consolation from the sweet fragrance of the flowers beside your bed, looking at the blue sky and clouds through your bedroom window, recalling happy days gone by, or dreaming of a brighter future? When we think about your illness and suffering, we cannot help but sympathise with you from the bottom of our hearts. In the hope that we may be of some help, we are sending this pamphlet to you. We hope you will read it at your leisure.

CONCERNING MEDICAL CARE

No one likes to become ill; of that we can be certain. While no one wishes to become ill, in some cases it is often already too late when the illness is discovered. Why is it that we must all suffer from illnesses which we dislike so much? Since human life is supposed to be filled with happiness, why does detestable illness plague us? When we think about this situation we cannot help but feel indignant.

Once we become ill we are confined to our beds. No matter how many beautiful treasures we may gather around us, they are of no avail at such a time. Although many dishes of delicious food are placed in front of us, we are not able to eat and enjoy them. Our sadness, caused by the inability to move about freely, deepens day by day and night by night and finally drives us to the depths of despair.

How disgusting this illness is! It can darken our lives without a moment's warning! Where do these unwanted afflictions come from?

Needless to say, where anything happens there is a cause. In the case of any illness there is always a cause. Therefore if we can find the cause of illness we can always find a way to treat it.

Medical science says that illness is caused by bacteria and various micro-organisms. Thus medical science has developed treatments for all our aches and pains. Tenrikyo, however, teaches that the cause of illness is the wrong use of the mind and therefore instructs us in the correct use of the mind and the way to purify it.

In the past these two schools of thought - the one called medical science, and the other Tenrikyo - were thought to be incompatible because they taught divergent views, but in reality the two should work together in order to save the patient. Nowhere in Tenrikyo doctrine can one find a passage which denies or rejects doctors and medicines. On the contrary, we are taught that a person who is ill needs to be examined by a doctor and to receive the proper medicine, thereby relieving the anxiety of the patient, his family, and his friends.

The best treatment is not only to give the patient complete medical care, but at the same time to give instruction in Tenrikyo doctrine. If we can cleanse the mind of the patient through faith, the struggle against illness will end in triumph. Thus we are furnishing this information concerning the concept of illness based on Tenrikyo doctrine to those who are receiving medical treatment at the same time. We wish to recommend the Tenrikyo way of cleansing the mind.

THE CAUSE OF ILLNESS ORIGINATES IN OUR OWN MIND

First of all we must ask a question. What does Tenrikyo teach as the cause of illness? The answer to this question is given in the following lines from the *Mikagura-uta*.

Seventh, Suffering comes from your own mind,
So you should reproach yourself.
Eighth, Though illness is so trying,
No one has ever known its origin.
Ninth, Until this time all of you, equally,
Have been ignorant of the origin of
illness.
Finally, This time it has been revealed.
The origin of illness lies in your own
mind.

These lines, which are taken from the latter part of the Tenth Chapter of the *Mikagura-uta*, Songs for the Service, were written by Oyasama, the Foundress Miki Nakayama, in the form of a counting song so that people could easily remember and understand them.

THE EIGHT MENTAL DUSTS

As you know, small specks of dust can be blown away by a simple puff of wind, but before a person is aware of it, dust may accumulate, adhere to a spot and become very difficult to remove. Similarly, mental dust, created by the wrong use of the mind, will gradually cloud the mind.

Therefore Oyasama enumerated the following eight mental dusts to guide us so that we need not make the wrong use of our minds and to help us to reflect upon our own actions.

The eight mental dusts:
Miserliness
Covetousness
Hatred
Selfish-love
Enmity
Anger
Greed
Arrogance

Originally there were no unfortunate events or happenings in human life. If there is an unfortunate event or happening now, it is the result of a little speck of dust in the mind. We are meant to sweep away the specks of dust from our minds and to live a joyous life, this being the intention and guidance of God the Parent. We are taught that all illness is an indication from God the Parent of a person's accumulation of mental dust and also a manifestation of His parental love whereby we are warned to sweep our mental dust away quickly.

Until now we thought that illness was only pain and suffering, but if we ponder over the matter a bit further, we can easily understand that illness is a sign of God the Parent's guidance and we may be able to see a ray of joy and hope. In this way we shall be able to sense a bright light shining in our dark and closed minds. This is the Tenrikyo concept of illness.

As we view our illness from the Tenrikyo standpoint and consider our own mental dust, we shall come to realise that this mental dust was indeed the very reason we became ill. As we become aware of our mental dust, we should apologise for our wrong use of mind and try to rectify the situation. By simply doing this, all the dust will be swept away. When our minds have been swept clean, every aspect of illness will naturally disappear. Concerning this sweeping, Oyasama wrote the following in the *Ofudesaki*:

'If only you have finished the sweeping of your mental dust, I shall work remarkable salvation.'

Ofudesaki III, 98

How vibrant a state of mind this is!

When a Tenrikyo member becomes ill, he should say, 'I received a good warning', or 'I received good guidance', and accept it with joy. He should immediately reflect upon his own mental dust and strive to overcome both pain and suffering caused by the illness. Based on the Tenrikyo concept of illness, we shall be able to live a joyous life as we renew our joy through faith.

Reading No. 32
Spiritual counselling in Tenrikyo

By HISANORI KONTANI [a Tenrikyo priest]

One day, a young couple came to visit me seeking advice. They confessed to me that they had decided to get a divorce after only one month of marriage. I was completely bewildered at this sudden decision, and as the husband explained I listened carefully.

'I became impotent on our wedding night and have been ever since, although I thought I had sexual capacity and desire before that night. We cannot understand why this strange occurrence has happened.

And my wife, thinking that I have deceived her about my impotency, is very upset and angry with me. We have tried our best in various ways to make a normal married life, but it just has not worked out. So we have decided to divorce.'

After the husband's statement, I considered this couple and their differences very carefully and came to this conclusion:

The wife appeared to be big and manly and had a very passionate nature like that of the orc, which is one aspect of the divine grace of *Tsukiyomi-no-Mikoto*.

On the other hand, the husband appeared to be a very timid and little man with female qualities like that of the turtle, which is one aspect of the divine grace of *Kunisazuchi-no-Mikoto*.

Furthermore, having made this observation, I also took the following into consideration:

God the Parent taught us that representing heaven as male and earth as female, He had created husband and wife. Nevertheless, in the above case the relationship between this husband and wife was quite contrary to that which God the Parent had intended. She was living spiritually in the sky and he, on the earth, and therefore this was not the natural and right situation to bring about rain. Because of such reversed stand in spirit, rain (the husband's affection) could not fall well to his wife.

I said to them: 'As far as the sexual problem is concerned, you need not get a divorce. You got married because of your love for each other. Is this not true?' They agreed. 'I am going to tell you the intention of God the Parent in order that you may receive His divine grace. Please listen carefully.'

I continued as follows:

'God the Parent had created the female spiritually and physically in order to take the role of *Kuni-toko* as the earth. And He gave to the male the divine name of *Kunitokotachi-no-Mikoto* and its role to stand (*tatsu, tachi*) on the base, which is the earth. Accordingly, the female is represented as the principle of the earth, and the male as heaven.

Therefore, when at first having sex, it is natural that the man be on top, as heaven, and the woman be on the bottom, as the earth. No matter how aggressive a woman may be, at first she cannot be on the top.

In your case, I believe that the position of heaven and earth is spiritually reversed.

God the Parent says that at the time of the creation of mankind, He gave the divine grace of water to the prototype of man. The water, symbolising one of the spiritual tendencies of men, is to flow into a lower direction. It should never rain from the earth to heaven.

The problem which you are now facing is indeed as if the rain or water, which is the man's love, is incapable of falling onto the earth, which is the woman.

If you both solemnly promise to God the Parent that throughout your lifetime you will live with the attitude of woman as the earth and man as heaven, God will be sure to manifest His blessing to you.'

They replied that they would follow sincerely the divine principle of God the Parent.

I then administered the Holy Grant (the *sazuke*) on the husband. After the prayer, I invited them to stay for the night at my church and they did so. (The Holy Grant is a prayer to God the Parent asking for His divine protection.)

The next morning, I asked the wife if there was any change in her husband. She shyly told me to ask her husband. The husband said to me, 'Such a tremendous miracle has happened to me...' and he smiled.

Ten months and ten days later, a cute baby boy was born to that couple, and they now have two more children.

READINGS FROM ITTO-EN
Reading No. 33
Ho-en: the Rokuman Gyogan prayer

Oh Light of Heaven and Earth!
    accept this humble act of service
as a means to worship Thee.
I have nothing else to offer,
for I have no virtue of my own.

I have searched for the root
of all the troubles of the whole wide world,
and I have found that it lay within my own heart.
It was from this knowledge
sprang this act of worship.

I therefore entreat
that I may serve in this manner,
and that this service may make
for the strengthening
of the moral foundations of our land.

I cling to Thee alone, Oh Light!
that protects the rocks
that lie at the foundation
of the eight provinces of our country.

May this act of mine help to fulfil
the desire of the great emperor Meiji,
who sang that all men the four seas over
are one brotherhood.

Reading No. 34
Itto-en statues
By FINN STEFÁNSSON

The statues of the founder of Itto-en (The Garden of Light), Nishida Tenko (1872-1968) and his wife, stand at the entry to the Itto-en village of Kosenrin near Kyoto. The statues were created by S. Kitamura in 1957; he also created the peace statue at Nagasaki. In this way Tenko-san (as Nishida is known) and his wife left the village physically on the last night of the year. On New Year's Day they returned when they were asked. This proved that they owned nothing, and that all belonged to the Light, not to individuals. All members of Itto-en also leave the village once every year in the summer to renew this spirit. In the statues the ascetic and humbly serving attitudes of the couple are emphasised. In 1950 Tenko-san had a mystical experience of the Light, i.e. God or the All-embracing, and founded Itto-en whose most important characteristics are to serve and not to own.

'There is bottomless wealth in owning or having nothing,' Tenko said. Inspired by several religions and philosophies, for instance Christian charity, Buddhist compassion, Tolstoy's thought, European idealism and communism, Tenko started his mission which is embodied in the statue: an introvert as in deep meditation, but in practical life also on extrovert to help others, in a manner reminiscent of a saint.

The ideal of owning nothing, according to a 1984 brochure from Kosenrin, applies to both the material, the intellectual and the spiritual spheres. 'A man stands at the roadside. Although he is an ordinary man he clearly lives in the providence of Light. Sometimes he stands with folded hands as in a prayer, as if he worships the Invisible. Sometimes he goes into other people's houses to order the sandals, to weed their garden, to fix the outhouse, or to empty their lavatories....

He is neither priest nor layman, but he has an unlimited amount of *fukuden* (the pure wealth of owning nothing) and he works. He is nourished by the Light and works not to live but to express gratefulness for the blessings he has received.... He does not believe in God or Buddha or Confucius, but realises that they are all inside the gates of *Funi-no-komyo* (The Light of Oneness).'

Reading No. 35
The morning walk from Kosenrin
By FINN STEFÁNSSON

The photo above shows members of the Itto-en village collective, Kosenrin ('Light Source Wood') during their morning walk to Kyoto to help people by doing the dirty and disliked jobs, for instance collecting refuse. Considering the Japanese attitudes to what they hold pure and impure they debase themselves deeply in solidarity with marginal groups. Along the road children greet the procession with a special greeting pressing the palms of their hands together.

Kosenrin was founded in 1929 and consists of 300 members (100 families), 80 buildings and some farm land. People there live extremely ascetically - their dwellings are not much larger than a *tatami* mat - they live without property and completely collectively as one big family who eat together in a dining hall they have in common, and they pray together. The fundamental ethos in this form of life is called *Senko-sha* ('the organisation to spread light').

Although Itto-en is small in terms of numbers, the example it has set, and the religious thinking it has developed, have given it a wider influence and it is one of Japan's best-known religious groups.

READINGS FROM SOKA GAKKAI [1960s]

Reading No. 36
The objective of the Soka Gakkai

The objective of the Soka Gakkai lies, first of all, in teaching the individual how to redevelop his character and enjoy a happy life, and in showing all mankind how eternal peace can be established, through the supreme Buddhism, the religion of mercy and pacifism. Through this supreme religion, a person can escape from poverty and live a prosperous life, if only he works in earnest. A man troubled with domestic discord will find his home serene and happy; and a man suffering from disease will completely recover his health and be able to resume his work. Through the power of the Gohonzon (the central image of worship in Soka Gakkai), a mother worried with her delinquent son will see him reform, and a husband who is plagued with a neurotic wife can have her return to normalcy. We often hear of a man whose business is failing and who, after being converted to Nichiren Shoshu, has a brilliant idea, or makes a contact with an unexpected customer and begins to prosper again.

Most people are afflicted with various problems - either spiritual, physical or material, but everyone who believes in the Gohonzon (the object of worship in Nichiren Shoshu) can solve any problem and achieve a happy life. Men who are timid or irritable can gradually become normal before they become aware of the change in their character.

The true intention of the Daishonin ('great saint', the title given by Soka Gakkai to Nichiren) is to save the whole world through the attainment of each individual's happiness in life. Consequently, members of the Soka Gakkai are actively trying to make, first of all, the Japanese people realise this great Buddhism as soon as possible. But there is no nationality in religion. Nichiren Daishonin made a wonderful prediction about seven hundred years ago to the effect, 'As the Buddhism of Shakyamuni found its way to Japan from India by way of China, conversely, Our Buddhism will return from Japan to India by way of China.'

Without a doubt, the Buddhism of the Daishonin will spread all over the East in the near future, and finally throughout the whole world. World peace as well as the welfare of individual nations can be achieved only when the true religion is made the basic thought. If you take this Buddhism as the guiding principle of your daily lives, the happiness of the individual will be closely reflected in the prosperity of the society in which you live.

Each country can achieve prosperity without any harm to, or discord with, any other country. This is the spirit of Kosen-rufu (propagation of Nichiren Daishonin's teachings) and the Nichiren Shoshu Soka Gakkai is positively striving to achieve this sublime purpose....

□□□□

Reading No. 37
'Vision of a peaceful world'

READINGS FROM SOKA GAKKAI [1992]

With members in 115 countries and regions worldwide, the Soka Gakkai International (SGI) is a worldwide organisation of Buddhist lay believers active in the fields of peace, culture and education. SGI was founded in 1975 to embrace the growing international membership of the Soka Gakkai ('value creating society') which dates from 1930. Daisaku Ikeda, third president of the Soka Gakkai, was selected as the first SGI president, a post he continues to hold.

The religious philosophy of Nichiren Daishonin (1222-1282), on which the activities of the SGI are based, places special emphasis on the sanctity of human life and, as a natural outgrowth of this, on peace. In the final analysis, however, lasting peace can only be realised by challenging and overcoming the inner impulse towards hatred and violence that exists within us all - what Buddhism terms the 'fundamental darkness of life'. It is this dynamic process of self-reformation - 'human revolution' - and the resultant rejuvenation of society that forms the core of SGI's vision of a peaceful world.

The promotion of cultural activities and exchange on an international scale is an integral facet of SGI's activities. Such exchanges, appealing to our shared appreciation of the universal human truths to which all cultural traditions give voice, can make important contributions towards increasing tolerance and understanding of our differences.

Education is the work of raising the youth who will shoulder the burden of the future. SGI has been actively engaged in educational activities based on the principles that education should be holistic, international in its outlook, and designed to unleash the creative potential of each student. Education for global citizenship - a merger of our natural love for place and nation with an awareness of global responsibilities - has been a consistent theme of SGI's activities in this realm.

Our world as we approach the end of the century is in a period of transition of enormous proportion. The challenges facing humanity in such fields as disarmament, environmental protection and human development are without precedent. So, at the same time, are the possibilities. The members of the SGI are dedicated to the task of working for a new era based on the universal values of human equality and dignity.

READINGS FROM RISSHO KOSEI-KAI

Reading No. 38

Rissho Kosei-kai:

Veneration

Veneration, which is one of the most important of Buddhist practices, consists in various acts through which believers express
their devotion and gratitude to the Three Treasures: the Buddha,
the Law, and the Sangha [the Buddhist community]. For members
of Rissho Kosei-kai, regular morning and evening sutra recitation
is one of the most significant acts of veneration.

Seated before their Buddhist altars at home, members read aloud
important passages selected from the Threefold Lotus Sutra.
Through this self-discipline, members express veneration not only
for the Three Treasures but also for their ancestors; and by reflecting
on the content of the passages from the sutra, they learn to expand
their circle of love and gratitude to include all beings, sentient and
non-sentient.

It is easy and natural for us to be grateful to those who nurture
and love us — parents, grandparents, brothers, sisters, aunts, and
uncles. It may be more difficult to feel the same gratitude to the
parents and grandparents of our grandparents, and still more difficult
to feel gratitude to the spirits of even more distant ancestors. Yet
all these lives are part of the unbroken chain of our own existence.
And when we look back on the evolutionary process that gave birth
to life on earth, which was originally filled only with melted lava,
metals, gas and vapour, and how life forms divided into plants and
into animals (which evolved gradually through insects, fish,
amphibians, birds, and mammals, and finally into man), we realise
also that wood, stone, metal, and all other substances and beings
in the world have the same ultimate ancestors as ourselves. Truly
all things in the universe are related and exist in interrelationship
with one another, permeated by the same life-energy of the Eternal
Buddha.

Through sutra recitation members become keenly aware of this
truth and of the necessity to express gratitude to one another and
to live together in harmony, with equal love for others and with a

feeling of unity. Although sutra recitation is an excellent expression of veneration to the Three Treasures, one's ancestors, and all beings, the highest expression of veneration is the practice of the way of the bodhisattva.

Reading No. 39

Rissho Kosei-kai:

Hoza: circle of compassion

One of the most important of Rissho Kosei-kai's activities is a unique form of group counselling known as *hoza*, which is guided by trained lay leaders. *Hoza*, whose origins are found in Shakyamuni's method of teaching his disciples, has been revived and emphasised by Rissho Kosei-kai in order to help people learn how to make practical use of the Buddha's teachings in everyday life. As in Shakyamuni's day, the counsel, tempered by compassion, benefits all the members of the group, not only an individual with a specific problem.

The members of a *hoza* group usually sit together in a circle, creating a warm, intimate atmosphere for open discussion. The spectrum of problems and questions raised in *hoza* ranges from personal problems at home or office, to problems of human relationships, questions of religion and ethics. As a member of the *hoza* circle speaks about his problem, the other members of the group listen and respond to him with compassion, trying to understand his emotions and his situation. When genuine sharing and mutual understanding are achieved, a troubled person very often expresses his true feelings, discloses his potential to attain enlightenment, and confesses his mental and physical misdeeds. Then together with the *hoza* leader the group works to apply the Buddha's teachings to the problem to gain insight and to find a solution.

The primary, and most important, aim of *hoza* is to help all the participants reveal and develop their buddha-nature by working together with compassion to solve the problems of someone who is troubled. When someone can truly realise that he has the buddha-nature, he comes spontaneously to recognise that others equally possess it. In *hoza*, participants try to find the buddha-nature in others; respect it as far as possible; and by doing so, make others become aware of it both in themselves and in others.

Since all beings are equal before the Law, each member of a *hoza* circle, especially the leader, should reflect on and confess his own misdeeds when considering the problems of another person because the surface of our buddha-nature is covered with various illusions acquired in the course of our daily lives. Through repentance, which purifies our minds and refreshes us because it relieves us of unwholesomeness, we attempt to remove such illusions from our buddha-nature; and through practice we can develop our buddha-nature.

Hoza, a manifestation of living Buddhism in action, differs from ordinary group counselling in several respects. First, the members of a *hoza* circle come together in a situation where they can practise the compassion taught by Shakyamuni Buddha and learn to extend it beyond that circle. Second, they learn to think of other people's suffering and problems as their own. Third, together they pray for a troubled person and seek for his problems solutions that are based on application and practice of the Buddha's teachings.

Members of *hoza* circles meet daily or weekly not only to learn how to employ the Buddha's teachings as a guide for living or to obtain relief from suffering but also to gain insight and to achieve spiritual growth.

Hoza 'circle of compassion'

READINGS FROM SEICHO-NO-IE
Reading No. 40

Holy Mission of *Seicho-No-Ie*

God the Almighty,
Viewed with mercy the sufferings of all men,
Appeared as a saintly being from Heaven,
Opened a universal Door of Blessings upon this
    earth,
And called it 'Seicho-No-Ie.'
Its holy mission is to bring enlightenment and
    salvation to all men.
Whether physical man or heavenly being,
Who could refuse to be helped by this teaching?

It matters not what one's religious belief is,
For this great benevolent teaching transcends all
    sects of all religions,
Erases all human suffering,
Destroys all sin,
And purifies all karma of all men.

When one contributes towards the building
    of temples, truth of life centres, and the like,
And, moved by Divine Love, he himself
    becomes a member of the Holy Mission Group
    in order to receive blessings not only for
    himself, but to bring salvation to all men —
He is one who has decided to enlighten all men
    to the Truth even before he fully
    comprehends the Truth himself;
And such a one could attain Bodhisattvahood.
Through merit thus gained,
He can clear the way towards the realisation
    of his Perfect True Image and the
    spiritual perfection in his nature.

Reading No. 41

Seicho-No-Ie:
Summary of the Teachings

The teachings of Seicho-No-Ie are summarised as follows:
(1) Man is a child of God. This is one of the most important points of the teaching. Man is really created in the image of God in the world of Truth, and already has the divine quality within himself, whether he recognises it or not. All we have to do is to manifest this perfect quality in this phenomenal world, then we can enjoy genuine happiness.
(2) The power of the Word is applied as a means of manifesting this indwelling infinite quality. For the Word is the Creator of the Spiritual Universe. (Here the Word implies Divine thought and Spiritual vibration at the same time.) Prayer and the recitation of Holy Sutras are other examples of the power of the Word.
(3) The phenomenal world duly reflects our own state of mind. If you wish to be really happy, therefore, you have to change your way of thinking.

According to whether your thoughts are dark or light, so your environment will appear, often concealing the real state of the Spiritual Universe. In order to be healthy, you must have harmonious thoughts and feelings. Here the law, 'Like attracts like' works exactly.
(4) In Absolute Truth, all religions are basically one and the same. This One Truth has appeared in different forms such as Christianity, Buddhism, Shinto and others according to differences in time, nationality and place.

We have to know the Oneness of Truth. Through this understanding, people will be united regardless of differences in their religion. This is one of the *raisons d'être* of Seicho-No-Ie.
(5) Deliverance from feelings of guilt which have concealed the divinity of the human race for a long, long time. With such a deep-rooted sense of sin, man can never be eternally saved. The mission of Seicho-No-Ie is to deliver humanity by letting them know that man is, in reality, a child of God and already immaculate and redeemed.

(6) Reconciliation, Perfect Harmony. Since our environment is the reflection of our mental state, as long as we possess deep-rooted discordant feelings, our inner perfection will never be made manifest in this world. Therefore, it is essential to reconcile ourselves with everyone and everything in the universe in order to experience genuine peace and happiness.

(7) *Shinsokan* (Prayerful Meditation). In order to realise oneness with God, Seicho-No-Ie teaches a unique meditation called *shinsokan*. This is also spiritually initiated through Dr Masaharu Taniguchi. Those who clearly realise their own divinity through this meditation can manifest their inner perfection through him. Numerous healings through *shinsokan* have been reported.

Reading No. 42
From Mahikari

How does Mahikari, the Divine Spiritual Radiation, change our daily lives?

If we continue to receive the Mahikari, our lives will change far more for the better than we ever expected in every aspect of our lives. For example, if a man suffering from a serious disease receives the *Mahikari no waza* [Mahikari's spiritual purification technique], he will regain his health rapidly without any additional medication. Another example - a man suffering from a long-term digestive ailment will be cured completely without any side effects by taking the *Tekazashi* [another name for Mahikari's purification].

The *Mahikari no waza* is not only good for illness but also for everything concerning your life including financial problems etc. Imagine you are in a financial crisis and you take the *Mahikari no waza*, believe it or not the situation will improve sooner rather than later. Even in relationships at work, you will be able to associate with others surprisingly better than before.

Nowadays particularly, there are crises among family members. If these families, however, take the *Mahikari no waza*, a truly harmonious and peaceful relationship will be restored. There will be no arguments or conflicts between husband and wife, parents and children or with in-laws. The family will begin to understand each other.

A man who often has accidents will not have any more. His spiritual rank will be upgraded so that every part of his life will simultaneously become joyful.

You may think that these examples sound fake but honestly speaking they are all true. Once you receive the Mahikari, you will see the difference and you will understand what the other miracles are all about.

Then the question might arise how Mahikari can solve these awkward problems. The power, Mahikari, purifies the spirits. This means that it purifies the roots of the problems right from the bottom. Yes, it is a spiritual purification. More than 80 per cent of everyday problems are caused by spiritual disorders.

The state of being possessed by spirits plays a major part in spiritual disorders, which cause serious diseases, poverty and family conflicts etc. When possessed by spirits, a man cannot give up worldly feelings like resentment or strongly negative feelings towards his family and friends. Our physical world's essence is the spiritual world. Thus, if you do not solve your spiritual problems you will never see satisfactory results in the physical world. We must solve our spiritual problems first.

Since the spirits have feelings, it is very difficult for them to forget what others have done to them, especially if they were murdered or their children were killed. Most of the spirits do not know that life is not only limited to this world but also exists in the astral and spiritual world. So their desire to plague others is stronger than their duty to go to the astral and spiritual worlds. But when they receive the *Mahikari no waza*, they will recognise their sin and see that those sins are related to what they are. They will understand the reason why they were murdered. The quality of their own dominant spirits is connected to their tragic end on earth. So receiving the *Mahikari no waza* is not only for the sake of your own spirit but also for those possessing spirits to be able to realise their sins and understand God's plan and guidance. Once those spirits become aware and go to the astral world, physical disorders are solved as if they had never existed.

God's true guidance, Mahikari, leads all spirits to their fundamental purpose, which is to establish heaven on earth.

7

Christianity in Japan

By IAN READER

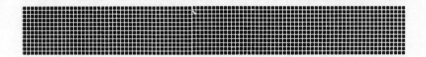

Buddhism, although it originally came from outside Japan, has become so firmly established in Japan as to be a Japanese religion in its own right. The other major religion to enter Japan from outside, Christianity, has not so far managed to do this, and continues to be somewhat distanced from the mainstream of Japanese religiosity. Christianity has never managed to adapt to the religious circumstances of Japan, in which cooperation and interaction between the various religions has been normal. Nor has it been able to come to terms with the importance of the ancestors in Japanese life, or with the fact that it is identified, by most Japanese, with foreign culture, with the result that becoming Christian can lead to an estrangement from the sense of Japanese cultural identity that is found in, for instance, Shinto.

For such reasons its following remains small, with little more than one per cent of the Japanese being adherents. Considering that Christianity first came to Japan over 400 years ago, and considering that a large amount of missionary work has been put into Japan by Christian teachers in the past century or so, this is a low figure. Indeed, there are some people, Japanese as well as Western Christians, who feel that Japan is simply not fertile ground for the spreading of Christianity. Some people have even voiced doubts about whether Christianity will survive in Japan at all.

It is true that, as we have seen in the previous chapters, the

Japanese have many alternative ways in which they can express religious feelings. However, despite its small numerical strength, Christianity has had some influences in Japan. Recent surveys have shown that many Japanese, especially young people, have warm feelings towards many of the ideals of Christianity, and have some knowledge of Christian teachings and of the Bible. To a great degree this is because of the growing influences of Western culture in Japan, and the increasing ties Japan has with the West. These have encouraged an interest in Christianity, and one of the results of Japan's rapid internationalisation is that many Japanese people are beginning to express an interest in the world outside of Japan and are keen to show that they have become internationally minded. Becoming Christian, or expressing an interest in Christianity, is one way of doing this.

Christianity's educational activities in Japan have encouraged this. Christian organisations have been active in establishing educational institutions and many of Japan's best schools and universities are today run by Christian organisations. Even though many of the students at these educational establishments are not Christian, they do encounter Christian teaching and ideals whilst receiving their education.

In addition to education Christianity has been active on the social front as well, and many hospitals and social welfare activities have been developed by Christians. Christian groups have also remained active and vigilant in seeking to guard against any return to the pre-war situation in which militant nationalism ruled the day, and one of the readings in the next chapter (on religion and politics) will demonstrate this.

Christian influences have also begun to appear in the new religions, as we saw in the previous chapter. In particular Christianity's concept of a Creator God, which is not found in traditional Japanese creation myths, has become common in many new religions. On more festive levels, too, Christianity has become widely known in Japan. Christmas, although not a public holiday, is greeted with all the seasonal trappings we know in the West: shops put up Christmas decorations and play Christmas carols, while models of the stable and manger are commonly seen in department stores and other places. At present, too, many Japanese get married in the traditional Christian white wedding style, either at a church or, more commonly, at a special wedding hall.

Despite this contemporary growth in interest in Christianity, however, the religion still is rather alien and foreign to most Japanese. This causes many problems for Japanese Christians, who often feel it hard to reconcile their belief in Christianity with their own cultural traditions. This is one of the issues discussed by Aasulv

Lande in the reading (No. 43) that follows. In this Lande provides an overview of Christianity's history in Japan and looks at the areas in which the different Christian traditions have been successful. He also shows that Christianity in Japan has not just been an imported religion wholly dependent on Western influences and teachers, but has produced many active Japanese Christian thinkers as well who have played a part in developing a truly Japanese Christianity.

Reading No. 43

Christianity's 'Three waves'

By AASULV LANDE

Compared to traditional Japanese spirituality, Christianity has a short and in many ways narrow history. Whereas Shinto, the Japanese national ethos, has developed out of the local cults, and Buddhism, Confucianism and Taoism were introduced together with Chinese civilisation in the first centuries of the Christian calendar, Christianity introduced itself as part of Western civilisation in the sixteenth century. It was, however, later banned but was reintroduced in the nineteenth century. Historians still ask whether it is rooted in Japanese soil, although it was perhaps unduly pessimistic for one of the greatest Japanese post-war church historians, Ishihara Ken, to claim that Christianity might once more disappear from the country.

Roman Catholics date the beginnings of Christianity in Japan to 1549, although many Protestants prefer to consider 1853, when Western influences returned to Japan, as the starting point. The 'Christian century' starting with the Jesuit mission from 1549 is seen as a prelude to this, while the new Christian initiatives after the Second World War are seen as renewals of old traditions.

This outline of 'beginnings' implies that Japanese Christianity in several ways is Western. It did develop largely as a response to

Western initiatives and Western ideals and thinking still prevail. However, the Western influence is decreasing, and in some churches missionaries are completely replaced by national workers; economics, administration and preaching are, with few exceptions, the responsibility of Japanese Christians.

The three waves

Christianity was introduced to Japan in three waves. When the Basque Jesuit missionary Francis Xavier and his helpers landed in 1549 in southern Japan, they represented the religious part of a Portuguese colonialist expansion across the seas from Africa via India and China to Japan. Religiously, the wave originated in the Roman Catholic counter reformation movement. For a brief period they were successful in converting Japanese people to their creed. But, as well as in the spiritual sphere, the 'Christian century' was dramatic at the political and diplomatic level and political worries and unrest in Japan led to a backlash against Christianity, which was banned and many of its followers executed. The increasingly harsh persecution of Christians from around 1600 onwards has offered the world a bloodstained image of early Japanese Christianity.

When the American Commodore Perry in 1853 forced Japan, through a show of naval force, to open her harbours and enter into a diplomatic and commercial relationship with the USA, a new era of Western-Japanese encounter dawned. In the wake of commercial treaties with Western nations, Roman Catholics re-entered the country, joining with joy and surprise the surviving remnants of the early Christians. Russian Orthodox missions as well as various Protestant groups also arrived, combining Christian the mission with Western education. A promising era of Christian progress in the 1870s and 1880s followed, but it was a transient phenomenon. In the life of a militarily and economically developing nation, Christianity was established as a minority comprising less than one per cent of the population.

The third wave of Christianity rolled over the Japanese islands as a result of the humiliating military defeat of the Imperial forces in 1945. After the Second World War, Christians were socially aware of the dangers of the Emperor system, and made serious efforts to develop social responsibility. Under the umbrella of the new, post-war constitution, which embodied cherished ideals of freedom, equality and democracy, Christianity once more progressed rapidly. But within a society achieving a miraculous recovery the progress of Christianity levelled off once again with about one per cent of the population becoming committed church members. New religions, rooted in traditional Japanese spirituality, however, met the religious needs of the people on a large scale.

Rejection and acceptance

Religious conversion and apostasy are irrational. But the total historical situation throws light also upon these deeply personal dynamics. There have been periods in Japanese history, when Christianity approached the status of a state religion. Such was the case in the early decades of Christian presence in Japan, when Oda Nobunaga rose to power. He persecuted Buddhist sects, which he regarded as contenders for political power. His support for Christianity can be interpreted as a part of his hatred for Buddhism. Positive relations with the missionaries also greatly facilitated trade with the Portuguese.

His positive attitude to Christianity was for some years continued from 1583 by his successor, Toyotomi Hideyoshi. The Japanese rulers, however, increasingly feared the dangers of European colonialism. New Roman Catholic orders and other European nationalities arrived besides the Portuguese Jesuits. The information stemming from mutual distrust between these groups certainly alarmed the supreme Japanese ruler. The Tokugawa supreme rulers (shogun) rose to power from 1600. Following increasing persecution during the early decades of the seventeenth century, Christianity was virtually uprooted in Japan by 1640.

The rejection of Christianity was not solely a political decision. Christianity was strange to the Japanese. The absoluteness of Christian claims contrasted with the warm, inclusive ambiguity of Japanese religiosity. Another religious reason for rejection was an apparent lack of divine protection in Christianity. In Japan, the Christian God seemed unable to save his adherents from pain and misery. The fate of the crucified Jesus himself underlined the argument. Alleged doctrinal and scriptural inconsistencies were also brought up in the religious encounters during the 'Christian century'.

Christians, however, believed that the pain of Christ was the entrance to heavenly glory. Christianity was believed to be the only road to glory and salvation. A central feature of early Catholicism, was the faith in Mary. Through this faith, partly transformed from popular veneration of Kannon in Buddhism, a warm, motherly flavour coloured the faith of early Japanese Christianity.

Japanese criticisms of Christianity generally follow the patterns already set by the critiques from the sixteenth century. The patriotic argument with its political dimension, the religious argument that Christianity differs from the pantheist inclusiveness of Japanese

157

religiosity, and the focus upon intrinsic rational conflicts, e.g. between divine compassion and omnipotence, recur. The criticism is also influenced by Western anti-religious criticism, and kindles strong national emotions even in the 1990s.

Believers have struggled with these arguments through a whole process of Christian 'japanisation'. In the 1890s, Christians worked hard to demonstrate to their fellow countrymen that they were Japanese patriots. In the period leading up to ultra-nationalism and fascism in the 1930s, Christians tried in many ways to demonstrate their patriotism. The ongoing process of indigenisation is in essence a Christian defence against the claims of the critics.

The warmth and inclusiveness of Christianity, which were shared by early believers, are sincerely cherished by Christians in the 1990s, particularly among Roman Catholics. The Catholic writer Endo Shusaku has focused upon such ideals. Many Roman Catholic priests from the West have also become involved in Zen meditation in attempts to combine aspects of Christian and Buddhist spirituality.

Protestants have particularly attempted to indigenise Christianity by social involvement and by seeking relevant expressions of Christianity in the modern Japanese situation. The ideals prior to the Second World War, to identify Christianity with Japanese developments, have been substituted by a more critical post-war involvement.

Catholic farmers and Protestant samurai

When Christianity was brought to Japan after 1853, the Roman Catholic and the Protestant starting points were very different. The Roman Catholic missionaries were largely involved with the fishermen and farmers from old Christian communities in Southern Japan. The Russian Orthodox Church and to a larger degree the Protestants were involved with the intellectuals. Samurai, also those who were outside the circles of political power, were interested in schools of Western learning. Classes of such samurai in Kumamoto, Sapporo and in Yokohama discovered in Christianity an inspiring basis for the building of a new, modern society. They also become the first Protestant leaders in Japan.

Japanese Christian personalities

While Christianity has never been a mass-movement in Japan, it has had many influences in Japanese society and has produced many exceptional leaders. In the period of modernisation during the Meiji period (1869-1912), there appeared several remarkable personalities, particularly in the samurai-led Protestantism. Protestantism taught the eternal value of the individual soul, and focused upon the conscience and individual responsibility. The moralism of Protestantism, including Sunday observance and a clear denial of ancestor-worship, was anti-communal in the Japanese society and hence demanded rugged individualism and personal independence. Such features apparently appealed to the lofty personal ideals and the leadership training of many samurai.

Particularly outstanding Christian personalities were Uchimura Kanzo (1861-1930), Ebina Danjo (1857-1937) and Uemura Masahisa (1857-1925), all of them of samurai background.

Uchimura Kanzo is particularly famous for founding the Non-Church Movement. At the Sapporo Agricultural School, where he specialised in agriculture, he became deeply concerned about the spiritual aspects of the new Japanese nationality. The entire class, among them Uchimura, was converted to Christianity, due to the influence of Dr W.S. Clark (1826-1886), an American agricultural educationalist. The Sapporo converts later formed their own church, outside Church denominations. Ideas of spirituality and independence were developed gradually by Uchimura into a Non-Church theology. This was not a denial of Christian fellowship, but of denominationalism. Uchimura called his fellowship a 'church' for the churchless. The ideal was a Biblical fellowship. His deep personal and spiritual understanding of Christianity and his concern for peace were rooted in a spiritual reverence for the Bible.

Ebina Danjo was influenced by the American instructor, Captain L.L. Janes, and was converted to Christianity whilst studying Western learning at the Kumamoto School. He later studied theology at Doshisha School, which was founded by the pioneer Christian educator Niijima Jo in 1875. Ebina was not only convinced that Christianity in Japan should build on Japanese traditions, but even held that Japanese religious traditions converged towards Christianity. He saw Christianity as a fulfilment of monotheistic motifs in Shinto. As a political philosopher, Ebina was convinced that Christianity was necessary for the development of Japanese democracy. Pastor Ebina focused on Christ as brother and transmitted powerfully the vision of the graceful Father.

The theology of his contemporary, the orthodox reformer Uemura Masahisa was classical Calvinist Protestantism. Uemura was an ecclesiastical leader, diligently working for Protestant unity and church independence. A samurai, brought up as a Christian believer in the missionary-led Yokohama school of Western studies, he emerged as the dominant leader of Japanese Protestantism in the 1890s. As an apologist, Uemura confronted rationalism and materialism, fighting for a Christian understanding of Western civilisation.

Modern trends in Japanese Christianity

A generation after the Second World War a distinct character of Japanese Christianity is apparent in Protestant as well as in Catholic circles. There is no astonishing church growth, Christianity still remains very much a minority religion but it has made the minority-situation an asset. Its smallness is its strength. The lines from the apologetic concerns of the early Catholic Christians and the call for Biblical purity in the scriptures of Uchimura converge in achievements such as the literature by Endo Shusaku or in the Protestant Theology of Pain, as formulated by Kitamori Kazo. The theme of both these achievements is the greatness of the divine disaster. In such ways Japanese Christianity remains active and continues to develop its own theology and outlooks on the world, thus contributing both to the world of Japanese religions and to Christianity in general.

8

Religion and Politics in Japan

By IAN READER

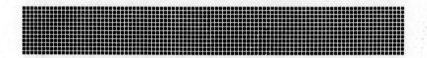

The close relationship between religion and politics, and between religion and the state has been one of the most constant, enduring and, at times, controversial, themes of religion in Japan. We have seen, for example, how the early Shinto myths recounted in Chapter Four provided support for the Imperial family and depicted a special relationship between the Emperor and the *kami*. It is not just Shinto, however, that has had a close association with the state and politics. Throughout its history Japanese Buddhism has been involved in political matters and has benefited from the patronage of the state, while many Buddhist leaders have sought a close relationship between their religion and the forces of political power. As we have seen, Nichiren was especially active here, seeking union between Buddhism and the state, an aim also picked up and promoted by the new religion Soka Gakkai.

The most prominent example of this union of religion, politics and the state was during the period of extreme Japanese nationalism that led to Japan's military expansion and war-like activities in Asia in the 1930s and to Japan's entry into the Second World War. From the latter part of the nineteenth century onwards Shinto was promoted as a state religion, to which all others were subservient. This system emphasised extreme nationalism and the veneration of and loyalty to the Emperor as the supreme symbol of Japan. It

161

The immense and elemental shape of Mount Fuji, symbol of Japan and Japanese spirituality (*see page 116*)

should be noted that it was not only Shinto that became involved in such nationalistic policies and attitudes. Virtually all Japanese religious groups, including the Buddhists and even many Japanese Christians, gave support to this militant nationalism in the period that the Japanese refer to as the 'dark valley' when their nation slid into militarism and war.

The Allied occupation of Japan legally put an end to the union of state and religion, and the current Japanese constitution affirms a complete separation of the two. Nonetheless, there remain some nationalist groups and people who would like to reaffirm the role of the Emperor as a *kami*, and to re-establish a bond between Shinto and the state. These moves are opposed by many in Japan, by many religious organisations as well as by liberal and left-wing political organisations, while perhaps the most vocal opposition of all comes from the small but well organised and active Japanese Christian groups.

READINGS

The readings in this chapter are arranged chronologically to give some idea of this issue as it has evolved in history. Because the relationship between Shinto and the state in the period up to 1945 has had such huge repercussions on Japanese life, most of the readings have centred on this issue and its results.

The first reading, No. 44, however, takes us back to the beginning of the seventh century, and to the first attempt to devise a written code of government for Japan. This is Prince Shotoku's famous 17-article constitution, in which the prince, heavily influenced by Buddhism and Confucianism, outlined his ideal principles of government along with the duties of its officials and the obligations of its citizens. Shotoku's constitution clearly affirms the importance of the ruler, enjoining all who hear imperial commands to scrupulously obey them. Yet it also promotes the Confucian ideal of harmony and benevolence, tempered also with Buddhist compassion and ethical behaviour. The rulers and their ministers are told to behave decorously and to avoid the abuse of power in any way. This combination of moral action and benevolent rule is aimed at the creation of harmony in all matters, and this ideal has been a constant theme expressed by all who have supported union between religion and the state in Japan.

Although the myth of Imperial and Japanese descent from the *kami* was written into texts such as the *Kojiki* it was not until the Tokugawa era, when a group of Japanese intellectuals and nationalists began to study again these ancient texts, that the idea of Japan as the chosen country of the gods became widely promoted.

Carrying three portable shrines on their shoulders, parishioners run down the stone stairway of Suwa Shrine, Nagasaki City, Kyushu, on 9 October to mark the beginning of the annual Nagasaki 'Okunchi' (dedication) festival of the shrine. The festival originated in 1634

The roots of nineteenth and twentieth-century Japanese nationalism can be traced back to this period and to writers such as Motoori Norinaga (1730-1801), from whose prolific works comes the second reading, No. 45. In this Motoori not only affirms the relationship of the Imperial lineage to the Sun Goddess but states clearly the notion that Japan is itself special, not just the source of all other countries but superior to them in every respect.

The Meiji era (1868-1912) marks the period when Japan, as well as opening its shores to the outside world, began to develop a modern nationalist state with the Emperor as its figurehead. Education and the schools were brought under direct government control, and became the arena in which the Japanese of successive generations were given a nationalistic education and were taught to venerate the Emperor. Reading No. 46 gives the text of the Imperial Rescript on Education promulgated in 1890 which outlines the principles of harmony and obedience to the state and Emperor on which the education system was based. The next reading, No. 47, also comes from the world of education, this time from a textbook on ethics issued by the Department of Education and in use in Japanese schools in the 1930s. The textbook aims to instil in pupils an unquestioning loyalty to the state, and in this extract makes use of Shinto mythology to do this by asserting the unity of state, Emperor and people.

With the war defeat of 1945 much changed. One early act of the Occupation government headed by the American General Douglas MacArthur was a directive to disestablish Shinto by separating it from the state and withdrawing from it such official support as financial aid from national and local government agencies. Reading No. 48 gives sections from the text of this directive, while the next reading, No. 49, is a translation of the statement made by the late Emperor Hirohito in 1946 in which he formally renounced the concept of his divinity as well as the notion that the Japanese were a superior race destined to rule the world.

This statement appeared to have buried for good the nationalistic ideas prominent in the earlier part of this century. However, although later constitutional provisions have legally separated religion and the state, there still are some Japanese who would like to revive the bond between Shinto and the state to proclaim anew the Emperor's divinity.

One particular area of contention is the Yasukuni shrine in Tokyo. This Shinto shrine was founded in 1869 to enshrine the spirits of those who had died fighting for the country, and has ever since been an important symbol of Shinto nationalism. There have been repeated attempts by nationalists to pass a special law enabling government funds to be used for its upkeep, while leading politicians

Yasukuni Shrine, Tokyo

have made formal visits to the shrine, including, in 1985, the then Prime Minister Nakasone. Such actions, which imply support for the nationalistic overtones of the shrine, have met with fierce resistance among many sections of the Japanese population fearful of a possible revival of the old-style nationalism.

Reading No. 50 presents the views of a Christian group opposed to what it sees are moves aimed at turning the clock back to the pre-war days. This reading has been chosen to illustrate the views and the worries held by some groups in Japan concerning the issue of nationalism and religion. It also, through its occasionally extreme language, shows how this issue remains a source of dispute and confrontation.

The relationship between religion, politics and the state, as these readings show, has been a very important thread in the overall picture of Japanese religions. Although in theory the reforms and constitutional changes made after the war would appear to have settled the issue at least in legal terms, it remains an issue of some importance which, as the last text clearly shows, continues to stir up emotions in Japan today.

Reading No. 44

The Seventeen-Article Constitution of Prince Shotoku

[I] Harmony is to be valued, and an avoidance of wanton opposition to be honoured. All men are influenced by partisanship, and there are few who are intelligent. Hence there are some who disobey their lords and fathers, or who maintain feuds with the neighbouring villages. But when those above are harmonious and those below are friendly, and there is concord in the discussion of business, right views of things spontaneously gain acceptance. Then what is there which cannot be accomplished?

[II] Sincerely reverence the three treasures. The three treasures, viz. Buddha, the Law, and the Monastic orders, are the final refuge of the four generated beings, and are the supreme objects of faith in all countries. Few men are utterly bad. They may be taught to follow it. But if they do not betake them to the three treasures, wherewithal shall their crookedness be made straight?

[III] When you receive the imperial commands, fail not scrupulously to obey them. The lord is Heaven, the vassal is Earth. Heaven overspreads, and Earth upbears. When this is so, the four seasons follow their due course, and the powers of Nature obtain their efficacy. If the Earth attempted to overspread, Heaven would simply fall in ruin. Therefore is it that when the lord speaks, the vassal listens; when the superior acts, the inferior yields compliance. Consequently, when you receive the imperial commands, fail not to carry them out scrupulously. Let there be a want of care in this matter, and ruin is the natural consequence.

[IV] The ministers and functionaries should make decorous behaviour their leading principle, for the leading principle of the government of the people consists in decorous behaviour. If the superior do not behave with decorum, the inferiors are disorderly: if inferiors are wanting in proper behaviour, there must necessarily be offences.

[V] Ceasing from gluttony and abandoning covetous desires, deal impartially with the suits which are submitted to you.

[VI] Chastise that which is evil and encourage that which is good. This was the excellent rule of antiquity. Conceal not, therefore, the good qualities of others, and fail not to correct that which is wrong when you see it. Flatterers and deceivers are a sharp weapon for the overthrow of the State, and a pointed sword for the destruction of the people.

[VII] Let every man have his own charge, and let not the spheres of duty be confused. When wise men are entrusted with office, the sound of praise arises. If unprincipled men hold office, disasters and tumults are multiplied. In this world, few are born with knowledge: wisdom is the product of earnest meditation. In all things, whether great or small, find the right man, and they will surely be well managed.

[VIII] Let the ministers and functionaries attend the court early in the morning, and retire late. The business of the State does not admit of remissness, and the whole day is hardly enough for its accomplishment.

[IX] Good faith is the foundation of right. In everything let there be good faith, for in it there surely consist the good and the bad, success and failure.

[X] Let us cease from wrath, and refrain from angry looks. Nor let us be resentful when others differ from us. For all men have hearts, and each heart has its own leanings. Their right is our wrong, and our right is their wrong.

[XI] Give clear appreciation to merit and demerit, and deal out to each its sure reward or punishment. In these days, reward does not attend upon merit, nor punishment upon crime. Ye high functionaries who have charge of public affairs, let it be your task to make clear rewards and punishments.

[XII] Let not the provincial authorities of the Kuni no Miyakko [local nobles] levy exaction on the people. In a country there are not two lords; the people have not two masters. The sovereign is the master of the people of the whole country. The officials to whom he gives charge are all his vassals.

[XIII] Let all persons entrusted with office attend equally to their functions.

[XIV] Ye ministers and functionaries! Be not envious. For if we envy others, they in turn will envy us. The evils of envy know no limit. If others excel us in intelligence, it gives us no pleasure; if they surpass us in ability, we are envious.

[XV] To turn away from that which is private, and to set our faces towards that which is public — this is the path of a minister. Now if a man is influenced by private motives, he will assuredly feel resentments, and if he is influenced by resentful feelings, he will assuredly fail to act harmoniously with others.

[XVI] Let the people be employed [in forced labour] at seasonable times. This is an ancient and excellent rule. Let them be employed, therefore, in the winter months, when they are at leisure.

[XVII] Decisions on important matters should not be made by one person alone. They should be discussed with many. But small matters are of less consequence. It is unnecessary to consult a number of people. It is only in the case of the discussion of weighty affairs, when there is a suspicion that they may miscarry, that one should arrange matters in concert with others, so as to arrive at the right conclusion.

Adapted from W. G. Aston, *Nihongi*, II, 128-33.

Reading No. 45
Motoori Norinaga: On the Emperor and Japan

Heaven and earth are one; there is no barrier between them. The High Heavenly Plain is the high heavenly plain which covers all the countries of the world, and the Sun Goddess is the goddess who reigns in that heaven. Thus, she is without a peer in the whole universe, casting her light to the very ends of heaven and earth and for all time. There is not a single country in the world which does not receive her beneficent illuminations, and no country can exist even for a day or an hour bereft of her grace. This goddess is the splendour of all splendours. However, foreign countries, having lost the ancient tradition of the Divine Age, do not know the meaning of revering this goddess. Only through the speculations of the human intelligence have they come to call the stars and the moon the spirit of yang and yin. In China and other countries the 'Heavenly Empire' is worshipped as the supreme divinity. In other countries there are other objects of reverence, each according to its way, but their teachings are based, some on the logic of inference, and some on arbitrary personal opinions. At any rate, they are merely man-made designations and the 'Heavenly Ruler' or the 'Heavenly Way' have no real existence at all. That foreign countries revere such non-existent beings and remain unaware of the grace of the Sun Goddess is a matter of profound regret. However, because of the special dispensation of our Imperial Land, the ancient tradition of the Divine Age has been correctly and clearly transmitted in our country, telling us of the genesis of the great goddess and the reason for her adoration.

The 'special dispensation of our Imperial Land' means that ours is the native land of the Heaven-Shining Goddess who casts her light over all countries in the four seas. Thus our country is the source and fountainhead of all other countries, and in all matters it excels all the others. It would be impossible to list all the products in which our country excels, but foremost among them is rice, which sustains the life of man, for whom there is no product more important. Our country's rice has no peer in foreign countries, from which fact it may be seen why our other products are also superior. Those who were born in this country have long been accustomed to our rice and take it for granted, unaware of its excellence. They can enjoy such excellent rice morning and night to their heart's content because they have been fortunate enough to be born in this country. This is a matter for which they should give thanks to our shining deities, but to my great dismay they seem to be unmindful of it.

Our country's Imperial Line, which casts its light over this world, represents the descendants of the Sky-Shining Goddess. And in accordance with that Goddess's mandate of reigning 'for ever and ever, coeval with Heaven and earth', the Imperial Line is destined to rule the nation for ever until the end of time and as long as the universe exists. That is the very basis of our Way. That our history has not deviated from the instructions of the divine mandate bears testimony to the infallibility of our ancient tradition. It can also be seen why foreign countries cannot match ours and what is meant by the special dispensation of our country. Foreign countries expound their own ways, each as if its way alone were true. But their dynastic lines, basic to their existence, do not continue; they change frequently and are quite corrupt. Thus one can surmise that in everything they say there are falsehoods and that there is no basis in fact for them.

Reading No. 46
Imperial Rescript on Education

Know ye, Our subjects:
Our Imperial Ancestors have founded Our Empire on a basis broad and everlasting, and have deeply and firmly implanted virtue; Our subjects ever united in loyalty and filial piety have from generation to generation illustrated the beauty thereof. This is the glory of the fundamental character of Our Empire, and herein also lies the source of Our education. Ye, Our subjects, be filial to your parents, affectionate to your brothers and sisters; as husbands and wives be harmonious, as friends true; bear yourselves in modesty and moderation; extend your benevolence to all; pursue learning and cultivate arts, and thereby develop intellectual faculties and perfect moral powers; furthermore, advance public good and promote common interests; always respect the Constitution and observe the laws; should emergency arise, offer yourselves courageously to the State; and thus guard and maintain the prosperity of Our Imperial Throne coeval with heaven and earth. So shall ye not only be Our good and faithful subjects, but render illustrious the best traditions of your forefathers.

The Way here set forth is indeed the teaching bequeathed by Our Imperial Ancestors, to be observed alike by Their Descendants and the subjects, infallible for all ages and true in all places. It is Our wish to lay it to heart in all reverence, in common with you, Our subjects, that we may attain the same virtue.

The 30th day of the 10th month of the 23rd year of Meiji.
(The 30th of October, 1890).
(Imperial Sign Manual. Imperial Seal).

First published, Dairoku Kikuchi, *Japanese Education* (London: John Murray Publishers, 1909).

Reading No. 47
Extract from a textbook on ethics from the 1930s

In ancient times Amaterasu-Ōmikami sent down her grandson, Ninigi-no-Mikoto, and caused him to rule over this country. The great grandchild of this prince was Jimmu Tennō. Since that time the descendants of this Emperor have succeeded to the Imperial Throne without interruption. From the year of the accession of Emperor Jimmu to the present is upwards of two thousand five hundred and ninety years [the book was published in 1930].

During this period our nation has had the Imperial Family as its centre and the entire nation has flourished like a single great family. The successive generations of Emperors have loved their subjects as children, and we subjects, beginning with our ancestors, have reverently obeyed the Emperors and have fulfilled the principles of loyalty and patriotism. There are many countries in the world, but there is no other which, like our empire of Great Japan, has over it an Emperor of one and the same dynasty throughout the ages, wherein the Imperial Family and the people of the nation are one body.

We who are born in such a precious country, who have over us such an august Imperial Family, and who, again, are the descendants of subjects who have bequeathed such beautiful customs, must become splendid Japanese and do our utmost for our empire.

From *Jinjō Shōgaku Shūshinsho* ("Textbook of Ethics for Ordinary Primary Schools"), Vol. V, pp. 1-2; Tokyo, 1930.

Reading No. 48

Directive for the disestablishment of State Shinto

Orders from the Supreme Commander for the Allied Powers to the Japanese Government [Extracts]

15 December 1945

MEMORANDUM FOR: Imperial Japanese Government
THROUGH: Central Liaison-Office, Tokyo
SUBJECT: Abolition of Governmental Sponsorship, Support, Perpetuation, Control, and Dissemination of State Shinto (*Kokka Shinto, Jinja Shinto*)

1. In order to free the Japanese people from direct or indirect compulsion to believe or profess to believe in a religion or cult officially designated by the state, and

In order to lift from the Japanese people the burden of compulsory financial support of an ideology which has contributed to their war guilt, defeat, suffering, privation, and present deplorable condition, and

In order to prevent recurrence of the perversion of Shinto theory and beliefs into militaristic and ultra-nationalistic propaganda designed to delude the Japanese people and lead them into wars of aggression, and

In order to assist the Japanese people in a rededication of their national life to building a new Japan based upon ideals of perpetual peace and democracy.

It is hereby directed that:

★ The sponsorship, support, perpetuation, control, and dissemination of Shinto by the Japanese national, prefectual, and local governments, or by public officials, subordinates, and employees acting in their official capacity are prohibited and will cease immediately.

★All financial support from public funds and all official affiliation with Shinto and Shinto shrines are prohibited and will cease immediately...

★The dissemination of Shinto doctrines in any form and by any means in any educational institution supported wholly or in part by public funds is prohibited and will cease immediately.

(1) All teachers' manuals and text-books now in use in any educational institution supported wholly or in part by public funds will be censored, and all Shinto doctrine will be deleted.

(2) No visits to Shinto shrines and no rites, practices, or ceremonies associated with Shinto will be conducted or sponsored by any educational institution supported wholly or in part by public funds...

★No official, subordinate, employee, student, citizen, or resident of Japan will be discriminated against because of his failure to profess and believe in or participate in any practice, rite, ceremony, or observance of State Shinto or of any other religion.

★No official of the national, prefectural, or local government, acting in his public capacity, will visit any shrine to report his assumption of office, to report on conditions of government, or to participate as a representative of government in any ceremony or observance.

The purpose of this directive is to separate religion from the state, to prevent misuse of religion for political ends, and to put all religions, faiths, and creeds upon exactly the same legal basis, entitled to precisely the same opportunities and protection....

★Militaristic and ultra-nationalistic ideology, as used in this directive, embraces those teachings, beliefs, and theories, which advocate or justify a mission on the part of Japan to extend its rule over other nations and peoples by reason of:

(1) The doctrine that the Emperor of Japan is superior to the heads of other states because of ancestry, descent, or special origin.

(2) The doctrine that the people of Japan are superior to the people of other lands because of ancestry, descent, or special origin.

(3) The doctrine that the islands of Japan are superior to other lands because of divine or special origin.

(4) Any other doctrine which tends to delude the Japanese people into embarking upon wars of aggression or to glorify the use of force as an instrument for the settlement of disputes with other people....

For the Supreme Commander:

[Signed] H. W. ALLEN
Colonel, A.G.D.
Asst. Adjutant General.

Reading No. 49

Imperial Rescript on the reconstruction of new Japan
[1 January, 1946]

Facing now a new year, we recall how, at the beginning of the Meiji Era, Emperor Meiji deigned to hand down the Charter Oath in Five Articles as the policy of the state.
He declared:
1. Conference shall be inaugurated widely, and all things shall be settled by public discussion.
2. Upper and lower classes shall be of one mind, and governmental administration shall be carried out vigorously.
3. Each and every person, in one and the same manner, beginning with the civil and military authorities and extending to all the masses, shall have opportunity to realise his aspirations, that the human spirit be not frustrated.
4. The evil practices of former times shall be broken down, and everything shall be founded on the just and equitable principles of nature.
5. Knowledge shall be sought throughout the world, that the foundations of imperial rule may be strengthened.
His majesty's wishes were impartial and just. What can we add to them? We herewith renew the oath and resolve on the promotion of the welfare of the nation. At all costs we must pattern our actions according to the spirit of the Charter Oath, we must leave behind the evil practices of former years, we must foster the will of the people, raise up government and people, and carry through in the spirit of peace, we must enrich education and strengthen the foundations of culture, and thus undertake the advancement of the life of the people and the establishment of a new Japan.
Cities and towns, large and small, that have sustained the ravages of war, the sufferings of an afflicted people, the stagnation of industry, the lack of food, the growing trend of unemployment — all this wounds the heart. Yet we doubt not that if our countrymen [waga kokumin], by squarely facing the ordeals of the present and by firmly resolving to seek civilisation through peace, bring this resolution to good issue, then not only for our country but also for

all mankind a bright future will open up.

Moreover, we know that the spirit of love of home and the spirit of love of country are especially strong in our nation. Now in truth is the time for expanding this and for putting forth sacrificial efforts for the consummation of the love of mankind. When we reflect on the results of the long-continued war which has ended in our defeat [*haiboku*], we fear that there is danger that our people find the situation hard to bear and that they sink to the depths of discouragement. As the winds of adversity gradually heighten, there is peril in the weakening of moral principles and the marked confusion of thought that they bring.

We stand together with you our countrymen. Our gains and losses have ever been one. We desire that our woe and weal should be shared. The bonds between us and our countrymen have been tied together from first to last by mutual trust and affection. They do not originate in mere myth and legend. They do not have their basis in the fictitious ideas that the emperor is manifest god [*akitsu mikami*] and that the Japanese people are a race superior to other races and therefore destined to rule the world...

Reading No. 50

Japanese Shintoism: the implicit resurgence of national religion

By THE NATIONAL COUNCIL OF CHURCHES (1984)

The recent political climate in Japan gives us the impression that Japanese history is moving in a reverse direction. As Christians, we are especially concerned about the movement by Shintoists to require the recovery of their old status as the national religion. Shintoism was the supreme religion in Japan which was placed above all other religions until the end of the Second World War and it was used as an organ of the oppressive rule by the government.

When state power is connected with religion, it often causes danger to the nation and people. It is what history has proven to us. Especially, we Japanese have experienced this teaching through our bitter modern history. Therefore, we fear the resurgence of National Shintoism would cause much danger in the future.

The Meiji government, which started Japan's 'modernisation', needed spiritual backbone or moral value to integrate the nation and chose the Emperor for that purpose. Moral support was especially needed to justify its military expansion to neighbouring countries. Shintoism, an indigenous Japanese religion, was used as the state religion for this purpose.

The people who died as a result of loyalty to the Emperor were also given special status as gods. The Yasukuni Shrine, which has about 2.5 million war-dead enshrined, was founded by the Meiji government. People who died on the battlefield for the nation and the Emperor were called heroic spirits (*Eirei*), and the Emperor himself worshipped them. Through these acts, Japanese people were compelled to think it was a great honour to be enshrined in the Yasukuni Shrine.

From the early 1950s, a movement has been taking place among former military personnel and the families of the war dead to nationalise the Yasukuni Shrine again. They want to glorify their dead for the nation. But their desire was taken over by the right-wing people and the Liberal Democrat Party (LDP) for their own purpose. Shintoists who organise the Shinto Political League are also in this circle.

The bill to nationalise the Yasukuni Shrine was first presented to the Diet in 1969. Since then, the LDP has presented the bill five times to the Diet. But, each time, it has not passed because of the strong opposition.

Meantime, the expansion of the Self-Defence Force (SDF) has gradually become related to Shintoism. The SDF has begun to help the enshrinement of their soldiers at the prefectural Gokuku shrines implicitly. In 1972, Nakaya Yasuko, a Christian widow of a SDF soldier refused the enshrinement of her husband, who was killed in a car accident while on duty, because of her belief that she did not want to deify her husband, a man whom she loved as a man. As the SDF did not agree with her, she is still continuing her court struggle for over eight years. She won at the district court, and the SDF appealed to the High Court, and the case is now in the Hiroshima High Court.

In 1979, the Yasukuni Shrine enshrined Class A War criminals who were executed by the Allied Forces. Among them, ex-prime minister Tojo. This act caused controversies not only among Japanese but also among other Asians. The officials of the shrine explained that these people had also dedicated their lives for the nation.

Recently, those who want to nationalise the Yasukuni shrine have changed their strategies again. They have organised local groups called *Eirei ni kotaeru Kai* (for the sake of heroic spirits) and are spreading the movement to require worship at the Yasukuni Shrine by the Emperor and the prime minister as 'official acts'. As the constitution prohibits religious activities by the state and its organs, these state officials say it is a private capacity when they visit the shrine. But the advocates of the nationalisation of the Yasukuni shrine want to change the word 'private' to 'official'.

In November 1980, these Shintoists celebrated the 90th anniversary of Emperor Meiji's Imperial Rescript on Education which emphasises loyalty to the nation and obedience to parents. This Rescript played a major role in pre-war education in developing Japanese into exclusive nationalists.

According to a leading Japanese newspaper in April 1980, a research organ of a Japanese business group issued a report on Japan's future, where it was stated that Shintoism should be used as the basis for national defence.

When we look at the present situation in Japan as described above, we have to recognise the danger of the connection between Shintoism and Japanese politics.

In 1982, the Japanese government decided on 15 August as a 'Memorial Day for War Dead'.

In August 1984, the government again organised an advisory committee on the worship of the prime minister and other cabinet ministers as the Yasukuni Shrine.

Prime ministers have changed their attitude as time has passed. First one claimed, 'It is a private visit', then, 'No comment'. The present Prime Minister Nakasone said, 'I have worshipped at the shrine, and I am prime minister', evading answering the question. It cannot be denied that this change has some relationship with the escalation of militarism in Japan which has come about since Mr Nakasone became prime minister. Thinking of this change in many areas of daily life, it is easy to presume that the advisory committee will lead to the conclusion which suits Nakasone's requirements.

Notes on the Readings

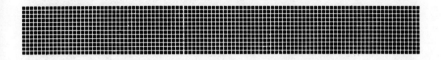

Many of the readings in this book have been written specially for the purpose, while others have been translated from Japanese sources, including brochures and cartoons, or have been based by the editors on such sources. A number have also been taken from existing Western language sources. The list below gives the sources for all the materials except those written specially for the book, and gives, where possible, the name of the author, the title of the original work, and the publisher:

Chapter 1: Meeting Japanese Culture

3. Harumi Befu *Japan - an Anthropological Introduction* pp. 166-170. Copyright © 1971 by Harper and Row, Publishers, Inc. Reprinted by permission of Harper Collins Publishers.
4. Ruth Benedict *The Chrysanthemum and the Sword* (Tokyo: Tuttle 1982) pp. 222-224. Copyright 1946 by Ruth Benedict. Copyright © renewed 1974 by Robert G. Freeman. Reprinted by permission of Houghton Mifflin Company. All rights reserved.
5. Takeo Doi *The Anatomy of Dependence* (Tokyo: Kodansha International 1973) pp. 48-50. Reprinted with permission. (*see p.32*)

Chapter 3: Folk Religion

6. Translation of a divination slip from Reizan temple.
7. Translation of a cartoon story about Kannon from Hase temple, Nara.
8. Translation of a popular cartoon about Jizo.

Chapter 4: Shinto

9. This selection of extracts from the *Kojiki* has been taken from

The Great Buddha of Kamakura. This bronze statue was erected in 1252 and weighs 210,000 pounds

the translation by Donald L. Philippi *Kojiki* (Tokyo: University of Tokyo 1968). Reprinted by permission of the author and publisher.

10. Daniel D. Holtom *The National Faith of Japan* (New York: E.P. Dutton 1938) pp. 22-25.

12. This text, originally translated by A.L. Sadler in *The Isle Daijingu or Diary of a Pilgrim to Ise* (Tokyo: Meiji Japan Society 1940) is given in H. Byron Earhart *Religion in the Japanese Experience: Sources and Interpretations* (Enrico, Cal., Dickenson 1974/Belmont, Cal., Wadsworth) pp. 25-26.

14. Translated by Donald L. Philippi in *Norito - a New Translation of the Ancient Japanese Ritual Prayers* pp. 45-49 and pp. 68-70. Copyright © 1990 by Princeton University Press. Reprinted by permission of Princeton University Press.

15. Daniel C. Holtom *The National Faith of Japan* pp. 160-161.

Chapter 5: Buddhism

16. Extract from a translation of the Lotus Sutra by W.E. Soothill *The Lotus of the Wonderful Law* given in R. Tsunoda, et. al., *Sources of the Japanese Tradition* (New York: Columbia University 1958) pp. 121-127. Reprinted by permission of the publisher.

17. This section is based on the section on *mandalas* in D. and A. Matsunaga *Foundation of Japanese Buddhism* Vol.1 (Los Angeles: Buddhist Books International 1974) pp. 184-193.

18. This reading is based on stories and legends found in popular Shingon Buddhist literature concerning the life of Kukai.

19. Translation of the text to a portrait of Kukai sold at the Shingon Buddhist centre of Koyasan.

20. Originally from H.H. Coates and R. Ishizuka *Honen the Buddhist Saint* (Tokyo: Kodokaku 1930) and given in R. Tsunoda *Sources of the Japanese Tradition* (see No.16 above) p. 208-209.

21. Originally from M. Anesaki *Nichiren the Buddhist Prophet* (Cambridge, Mass, Harvard University Press 1916) these texts are given in R. Tsunoda (see No. 16 above) pp. 225 and 230.

22. Aage Marcus *Den Blaa Drage* (1969) pp. 93-94.

23 and 24. These were originally published in Danish in the journal *Stupa* No.3 1980.

25. These *haiku* come from R.H. Blyth (trans.) *Haiku* (4 vols) (Tokyo: Hokuseido Press 1949). Reprinted by permission of the publisher.

27. Eugen Herrigel *Zen in the Art of Archery* (London: Routledge and Kegan Paul 1982) pp. 46-48 and 85-86. Translation © 1953 by Routledge and Kegan Paul. Reproduced by permission of Penguin Books Ltd. Copyright © 1953 by Pantheon Books Inc. in the

U.S.A. Reprinted by permission of Pantheon Books, a division of Random House, Inc.

Chapter 6: The New Religions

28. Tenrikyo *Ofudesaki* (Tenri: Tenrikyo 1983) pp. 146-152.
29. Tenrikyo *The Life of Oyasama, Foundress of Tenrikyo* (Tenri: Tenrikyo 1978) pp. 1-7.
30. Tenrikyo Overseas Misson *Oyasato* (brochure published by Tenrikyo, 1975).
31. Tenrikyo Overseas Mission *To All Our Ailing Friends* (Tenri: Tenrikyo 1978) pp. 1-3, p. 6, pp. 10-11.
32. Hisanori Kontani is a Tenrikyo priest, and the testimony he gives here is given in *Tenrikyo — Husband, Wife and Health* (Tenri: Tenrikyo 1985) pp. 49-53.
33, 34, 35. From pamphlets distributed by Itto-en, Kyoto.
36. This reading comes from a Soka Gakkai text. (Tokyo: The Seikyo Press, 1966). Reprinted with permission.
37. This reading comes from a 1992 booklet entitled 'Soka Gakkai International' with the approval of NSUK (associated with SGI).
38 and 39. From information materials and brochures handed out by Rissho Koseikai, Tokyo 1984.
40 and 41. From information materials and brochures handed out by Seicho-no-Ie, Tokyo 1984.
42. From information materials and brochures handed out by Mahikari, Tokyo 1984.

Chapter 8: Religion and Politics

44. The text of Shotoku's constitution is given in W.G. Aston (trans) *Nihongi: Chronicles of Japan from the Earliest Times to 697 A.D.* (Tokyo: Tuttle 1972) pp. 128-133.
45. This text is given in R. Tsunoda (see No.16 above) pp.522-523.
46. This text is given in R. Tsunoda (see No.16 above) pp.646-647.
47. This text is given in Daniel Holtom (see No.10 above) p.132.
48. This text is given in D.C. Holtom *Modern Japan and Shinto Nationalism: A Study of Present-day trends in Japanese Religions.* (New York: Paragon Book Reprint Corp. 1963) Reprinted with permission.
49. This text is given in H. Byron Earhart (*Religion in the Japanese Experience* (Belmont Cal., Wadsworth 1974). Reprinted by permission of the publisher.
50. This text was produced in 1984 by the National Council of Churches of Japan as part of their campaign against the moves to restore the Yasukuni shrine to its former status.

Bibliography

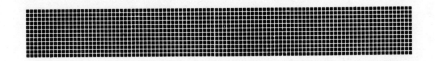

History and Culture

E. O. Reischauer. *The Japanese.* Cambridge, 1978.
E. O. Reischauer. *Japan - Past and Present.* Tokyo, 1980.
E. O. Reischauer and A. M. Craig, *Japan: Tradition and Transformation.* Tokyo, 1981.
G. B. Sansom. *A History of Japan I-III.* London, 1965-66.
G. B. Sansom. *Japan: A Short Cultural History.* Tokyo, 1981.
Encyclopedia of Japan. Kodansha, Tokyo, 1983.
Masaharu Anesaki. *Art, Life and Nature in Japan.* Tokyo, 1983.
Ruth Benedict. *The Chrysanthemum and the Sword.* London, 1967.
Harumi Befu. *Japan - an Anthropological Introduction.* Tokyo, 1971.
Takeo Doi. *The Anatomy of Dependence.* Tokyo, 1973.

General Works on Religion

Ian Reader. *Religion in Contemporary Japan.* London, Macmillan 1990.
Japanese Religion. A Survey by the Agency for Cultural Affairs. Tokyo, 1972.
J. M. Kitagawa. *Religion in Japanese History.* New York, 1966.
H. Byron Earhart. *Japanese Religion: Unity and Diversity.* Belmont, California, 1969.
R. Tsunoda, ed. *Sources of the Japanese Tradition.* New York, 1958.
H. Byron Earhart. *Religion in the Japanese Experience.* 1974.

Folk Religion

Ichiro Hori. *Folk Religion in Japan.* Chicago, 1968.

R. J. Smith. *Ancestor Worship in Contemporary Japan*. Stanford, 1974.
Tokihito Oto. *Folklore in Japanese Life and Customs*. Tokyo, 1963.
Carmen Blacker. *The Catalpa Bow, A Study of Shamanistic Practices in Japan*. London, 1975.

Shinto

D. C. Holtom. *The National Faith of Japan*. London, 1938.
S. D. B. Picken. *Shinto - Japan's Spiritual Roots*. Tokyo, 1980.
Sokyo Ono. *Shinto - the Kami Way*. Tokyo, 1962.
J. J. Spae. *Shinto Man*. Tokyo, 1972.
Jean Herbert. *Shinto: The Fountainhead of Japan*. London, 1967.
The Kojiki: Records of Ancient Matters. Translated by B. H. Chamberlain, Tokyo, 1981.
Nihongi. Translated by W. G. Aston, Tokyo, 1972.
Norito - a New Translation of the Ancient Japanese Ritual Prayers, by D. L. Philippi. Tokyo, 1959.

Buddhism

D. and A. Matsunaga. *Foundation of Japanese Buddhism I-II*. Tokyo, 1974 and 1976.
C. Eliot. *Japanese Buddhism*. London, 1935.
E. Steinsilber-Oberlin. *The Buddhist Sects of Japan*. London, 1938.
S. D. B. Picken. *Buddhism, Japan's Cultural Identity*. Tokyo, 1982.
E. D. Saunders. *Buddhism in Japan*. Tokyo, 1972.
S. Watanabe. *Japanese Buddhism*. Tokyo, 1964.
S. B. Dasgupta. *An Introduction to Tantric Buddhism*. Calcutta, 1958.
G. Tucci. *The Theory and Practice of the Mandala*. New York, 1969.
Y. S. Hakeda. *Kukai, Major Works*. New York, 1972.
H. H. Coates and R. Ishizuka. *Honen, the Buddhist Saint, His Life and Teaching*. Kyoto, 1949.
D. T. Suzuki. *Shin Buddhism*. New York, 1970.
A. Bloom. *Shinran's Gospel of Pure Grace*. Tucson, 1975.
M. Anesaki. *Nichiren, the Buddhist Prophet*. 1949.
Daishonin Nichiren. *The Major Writings of Daishonin Nichiren, 1-2*. Tokyo, 1980-82.

Zen

E. Wood. *Zen Dictionary*. Tokyo, 1982.
D. T. Suzuki. *Zen Buddhism*. 1962 (1985).

Alan W. Watts. *Zen Buddhism.* 1962 (1972).
R. H. Blyth. *Haiku 1-4.* Tokyo, 1949-52.
D. T. Suzuki. *Zen and Japanese Culture.* Princeton University Press, 1973 (1959).
G. Sato and E. Nishimura. *Unsei - a Diary of Zen Monastic Life.* University of Hawaii Press, 1973.
H. Dumoulin. *A History of Zen Buddhism.* Boston, 1963.
H. Dumoulin. *Zen Enlightenment; Origins and Meaning.* New York, 1979.

New Religions

Harry Thomson. *The New Religions of Japan.* Tokyo, 1963.
H. N. McFarland. *The Rush Hour of the Gods.* New York, 1967.
H. Byron Earhart. *The New Religions of Japan.* A Bibliography of Western-Language Materials, 1983.
C. B. Offner and H. van Straelen. *Modern Japanese Religions with Special Emphasis upon their Doctrines of Healing.* Leiden, 1963.
Tenrikyo
An Introduction to Tenrikyo: Its History and Teachings. Ed. by Tenrikyo Overseas Mission Department. 1966, (1978).
H. van Straelen. *The Religion of Divine Wisdom.* Tokyo, 1957.
Soka Gakkai
N. S. Brannen. *Soka Gakkai: Japan's Militant Buddhists.*
John Knox Press, Virginia, 1968.
Daisaku Ikeda. *Buddhism: The First Millennium.* Tokyo, 1982.
Seicho-No-Ie
Masaharu Taniguchi. *Truth of Life.* California, 1979.
R. E. Davis. *Miracle Man of Japan.* Lakemont, 1970.
Rissho Kosei-kai
Kenneth Dale. *The Circle of Harmony.* 1971.
Mahikari
Winston Davis. *Dojo: Magic and Exorcism in Modern Japan.*
Stanford University Press, California, 1980.

INDEX

INDEX